71

("Tu es venu et tu as vu.
Et, maintenant, le monde est
dans tes yeux." Reb Ibram)

Le rien peut-il enfanter un livre ? Là où se sont
évanouis les vocables, peut-on ~~retracer les~~ le ~~~~
d'une écriture ? ~~Sûrement~~, Dans la blancheur
ainsi la parole blanche, minuscule et muette, la
parole à jamais ~~~~ imaginée ?
    C'est en moi que les mots ~~~~ veillent, c'
est en moi que ~~tu~~ peux, désormais, lire le livre
des ~~branches~~ ~~~~ mots)
    C'est en moi ~~seul~~ que, ~~~~, s'épanouit le silence
aux déptiques.

    (" La fleur reprend toute
    parole qui ~~~~ ternie sa
    couleur."
            Reb Halfan

    " Le pétale est proche
    de la ~~~~ parole
    par le parfum et la
    couleur."
            Reb Calef)

Ceci est le vrai matin cendré, encore une journée morte
et le désert tel une parole imprononçable dans la
forge sèche.

Ceci M ~~l'immense~~ (plaie) ~~de sable~~ ~~de la parole~~ des ~~drap~~
~~dépliée~~ avec le désert, hérit-je des hébreux

"Tu peux bâtir ta maison avec les matériaux
les plus solides — écrivait Reb Alem — elle reposera
toujours sur le sable."

Et Reb Saadia: "Dans mes mains pleines de
sable, ô mon frère, je crois baiser ton visage"!

~~Ceci est le désert aux~~ ~~paris~~ ~~horizons~~ ~~du matin~~
~~Je pensais avoir~~ ~~abandonné~~ atteint la vallée
~~Je ne suis pas très~~ ~~lointain~~, le désert ~~vers~~ m'a
devancé." Disait Reb Faïz.

Ceci est ta mémoire morte, Sarah, d'où ~~a gelé~~
le cou solitaire dans lequel ~~où se~~ blottit un peuple ~~battant frileux~~
pour mourir ~~de~~ ~~faim~~
pour ~~retrouver~~ et se sacrifier.

Cette longue marche sans mémoire, entre ciel
et sable: de loin en loin, les mots ~~d'un~~ livre
~~détachés~~ de la phrase, ~~parfois~~ de la page, livrés à
leur origine; (détachés)

Ainsi l'oiseau est le premier oiseau, le ciel
est le premier ciel, chaque grain de sable, le

Quelle fut ta vérité, Yukel, à ce moment là où
telle fut celle de Sarah ?

Ta vérité était une blessure,
~~la vérité~~ de Sarah, une blessure ;
~~comme~~ ~~celle~~ de tous les survivants dont tu
affirmas le nom en retrouvant le tien.

La seule vérité était le mal subi et c'est
en fonction de ce mal et de cette vérité que tu allais
~~ajouter~~ la vérité universelle qui referait de toi
un homme,

par l'âme et par l'esprit.

(" Nos plaies sont des questions ~~désespérant~~ ouvertes — disait
Reb Simeon — ~~telles~~ ~~pareil~~ traçant nos chemins
Et Reb Aklé : Tu ignores ma douleur
comment veux-tu que je partage
ta vérité ? ")

Tu ne ~~pouvais~~ être libre que pour ~~les~~
de meilleur ~~en~~ ~~ou~~ de plus déchiré. C'est la liberté
des saints.
Il fallait que le monde ~~fût libre~~ fût à la taille de ton
corps et de ton âme meurtris.
à la mesure de meilleur et de plus déchiré de
ta vie vécue
afin que ~~un avenir~~ ~~te soit~~ ~~tu allais~~ ~~être~~ ~~peut-être~~
en harmonie avec tes gestes et tes
regards.

Vaut-il... la premier fustini à fait, de lui, un être libre, par
liberté [...] dire qu'il l'épanouissement d'un être, n'[...]
fleur fermée. tant [...] baignés le
long des siècles [...] ses pétales [...] disait Reb Totte.

[...] Reb [...] "Bottin" [...] répond: La fleur ne fleu-
au froid des profferes. Et celle qui s'ouvre [...] elle ses
prémices et ses douceurs. [...] Elle se sembl
jaunit, [...] de la mort qu'elle s'épa-
[...] la liberté [...] et dans le livre.

" Tu as voulu, Seigneur, [...] ta liberté et
ton [...] la liberté [...]
Ainsi, ton liberté, refuse sa vie volonté. Et
l'application d'un privilège que tu ne pouvons fixer." suivant Reb K

Mais ce Rabbin fut longtemps
combattue puis réduit au silence

" J'ai péché, sans doute, dans ton enseignem
conservait-il ailleurs — car [...] liberté
été liberté de Dieu seul. Mais comment ne
[...] pouvoir de [...] Seigneur
fils [...] Dieu [...]
conquis [...] que [...]

[...]
La liberté peut naît [...]
[...] deux volontés égales,
[...] dans l'accomplissem
ou des rejet d'une même promesse.

d'S. Souffrance

Dieu ~~est~~ le multiple de ~~ces~~ nombre Un, c'est l'unité ~~subordonnée~~ 38

La liberté du juif ~~ne peut être que la liberté~~ ou
la libre disposition ~~du juif~~ son être ~~peut-il~~
revendiquer en marge et dans la société.

Ainsi, les pages de mon livre. (Hors et dans l'~~œuvre~~)

Quelle est la force qui les inspire et la lumière qui
les éclaire ?

Je vis dans la nuit parmi ~~des millions~~
de créatures ~~inc~~ méconnaissables. Le soleil se lève
et se couche sur un autre continent.

" D'où viens-tu, mon frère ?

— De ma vie blessée.

— Où vas-tu, mon frère ?

— Vers une vie blessée. Reb ~~fémin~~ ~~perpétuelle~~
~~perpétuelle~~ ?

" Ah ! se peut-il que la vie soit ~~terrible~~ ?
Je le tiens de mon père et je l'ai transmise
à mon fils :— disant Reb Eloth. le plus ~~désespéré~~
~~malheureux~~ des enfants de Dieu.

~~Mais~~ il lui fut répondre que ~~cache~~ ~~dieu~~ la
plus aride peut un jour, grâce au courage ~~et~~
la persévérance de l'homme, ~~devenir~~ être ; en
tous, fertilisée.

~~Vers le jour et vers demain.~~

Et Reb Eloth ~~expira~~ poursuivit. Je garde de la terre,
un cruel souvenir, car les êtres ~~que~~ des que j'ai
vu périr ont été reçus dans son sein comme des parias.
Nous mourons à la tâche sans ~~jamais~~ ~~avoir~~ ~~vu leur~~ visage.

Yukel, tu es né de ma parole et tu ne l'as rendue
Ma parole à Yukel tous ses ... et ses ...
Écrit ma parole en deuil, le ... de tes livres
Ma parole sans avenir, perdue à la mémoire

" Yukel. Quelle est cette parole que tu ...
toi et de Yukel ; ...
Toi qui n'est pas Yukel dans la mesure où tu es
d'abord un homme
Toi qui ... Yukel par la parole ... rendue
et par le ... de tes écrits..? "

— Je vous parlai du "Livre des Questions".

" L'univers ... au seuil du livre — disait Reb
Armand — ..., il n'y a que des ...
en ... de l'univers.
Ainsi ... les juifs: ...

Et ... (... les yeux, ils ont
trouvé le monde ... promis. ...
ils ... maintenant ... ils cherchent "

Q.

Q. .

Q. . .

Q. . . .

. . . .Q

Q. . . . . .

Ques-
tion-
ing
Warren F. Motte, Jr.
Ed-
mond
Jabès

University of Nebraska Press

Lincoln & London

Acknowledgments
for the use
of previously
published material
appear on pp xi–xii

The paper in this
book meets the mini-
mum requirements
of American
National Standard
for Information
Sciences – Perma-
nence of Paper for
Printed Library
Materials,
ANSI Z39.48-1984.
Library of Congress
Cataloging in
Publication Data
Motte, Warren F.
Questioning
Edmond Jabès /
Warren F. Motte, Jr.
p. cm.
Bibliography: p.
Includes index.
ISBN 0-8032-3125-3
(alkaline paper)
1. Jabès, Edmond –
Criticism and
interpretation.
I. Title.
PQ2619.A112Z76
1990
848'.91407 – dc20
89-14642 CIP

For Jean Alter
and
Gerald Prince

c o n t e n t s

Questioning Edmond Jabès: the participle is deliberately equivocal. It is intended to figure two orders of inquiry, both Jabès's writing
and my reading of Jabès, for the Jabesian book, granted its dimensions,
its elliptical character, and its insistence on paradox and outright contradiction, defies familiar strategies of reading. One is obliged to elaborate fresh strategies to approach this body of work, and that is what I
have attempted to do, largely following the canny swerves and odd

profiles of the text itself. I have tried to trace various lines of questioning through Jabès's work, in a manner which is itself interrogative. I
have made considerable use of textual citation, hoping to coerce the
Jabesian text into reading itself, in a sense; hoping in any case to enlist
the text concretely in my efforts to make meaning.

The readings in this volume are highly idiosyncratic. The logic that
animates them derives in part from the singular, elegant tautologies of
Jabès's writing (in glossing those structures I find that I have often
recapitulated them). In part also, it must be admitted, it derives from
whim: after reading and rereading Jabès, from beginning to end and
from end to beginning, I chose to pursue those problems that most
piqued my curiosity. This being true, I have tried to organize my
readings in such a way as to present a coherent (though obviously
nonexclusive) itinerary through the Jabesian book. Thus the first chapter deals with what I consider to be the first, elemental question posed
by Edmond Jabès's writing, the question of legibility. There, grappling
with the widely held critical position that proclaims these books radically illegible, I have attempted to tease out and render explicit the
conditions of legibility that the Jabesian text postulates. In the middle
four chapters, I have examined a functional hierarchy that Jabès himself
proclaims, a structure whose base is defined by the individual, precombinatory letter, which progresses through the word and the story to
culminate in the book, the most highly determined construct in Jabès's
considerable catalog of metaphor. In the final chapter, I have considered the figures that Jabès proposes for his work, the circle, the point,
and the center; it is through these figures that he furnishes his remarkable literary space.

I have not hesitated to fall into anachrony. If I have often invoked *Le Livre
des questions* (1963) to help me read *Le Livre du partage* (1987), for
instance, I have equally often turned the latter upon the former. This
procedure, very questionable in the case of most writers, is justifiable
and even essential in Jabès's case, I believe, for his oeuvre elaborates a
lifework that transcends the individual book. Thus the seven-volume

Livre des questions resonates strongly in the *Livre des ressemblances* trilogy; each text describes both an eccentric movement and a movement of return to the texts that precede it; and the cycles of works in Jabès's writing cohere and inform each other. Through each book, Jabès is straining toward the Book. Therefore, I have regarded the individual texts in Jabès's work more as chapters in a more ample book and have considered them, after the initial act of reading, in synchrony.

I have done my best to respect the alterity of the Jabesian text, trying to do no more violence to it than strictly necessary. The tremendous "otherness" that characterizes Jabès's writing, as solid and powerful as it may be within the text, becomes far more fragile in the critical act. If reading necessarily entails a process of appropriation, it is important (crucially important in the case of this body of work) to minimize that process, to avoid each temptation to appropriate the text, insofar as possible. Reading Jabès is a lesson in humility: he quickly teaches one that interpretation cannot pretend to circumscribe the book, any more than the book can pretend to circumscribe experience. I should like to propose my readings, then, in a tentative manner. I hope that they demonstrate some of the openness of candid inquiry rather than the false closure of the answer. For how can one legitimately approach this extraordinary writing if not through a process of questioning?

ACKNOWLEDGMENTS

A version of "The Story" was published as "Questioning Jabès" in *French Forum* 11, no. 1 (1986): 83–94; reprinted with permission. The chapter titled "The Letter" appeared in the *Romanic Review* 77, no. 3 (1986): 289–306, as "Literal Jabès," reprinted by permission from the *Romanic Review*, copyright © by the Trustees of Columbia University of the City of New York. "The Word" was published in *Symposium* 41, no. 2 (1987): 140–57, as "Jabès's Words," reprinted with permission of the Helen Dwight Reid Educational Foundation, published by Heldref Publications, 4000 Albemarle St., N.W., Washington, D.C. 20016, copyright © 1987. I thank the editors and publishers of these journals for permission to use this material.

I am indebted to Sandy Adler for her patient, painstaking help in preparing the manuscript. I am deeply grateful to Arlette and Edmond Jabès for their kindness and their generosity; the encouragement they offered at every stage of this difficult project was vitally important to me. Finally, I should like to thank my friends Marie, Nicholas, and Nathaniel: this books is theirs, too.

A	*Aely* (1972)
BD	*Je bâtis ma demeure* (1959; 1975)
BQ	*The Book of Questions* (1976)
BY	*The Book of Yukel, Return to the Book* (1977)
CS	*Ça suit son cours* (1975)
DD	*Dans la double dépendance du dit* (1984)
DG	*The Book of Dialogue* (1987)
DL	*Du désert au livre* (1980)
E	*Elya* (1969)
EL	*•(El, ou le dernier livre)* (1973)
II	*L'Ineffaçable l'inaperçu* (1980)
LB	*The Book of Questions: •El, or the Last Book* (1984)
LD	*Le Livre du dialogue* (1984)
LP	*Le Livre du partage* (1987)
LQ	*Le Livre des questions* (1963)
LR	*Le Livre des ressemblances* (1976)
LY	*Le Livre de Yukel* (1964)
MM	*La Mémoire et la main* (1987)
P	*Le Parcours* (1985)
PL	*Le Petit Livre de la subversion hors de soupçon* (1982)
R	*Récit* (1981)
RL	*Le Retour au livre* (1965)
SD	*Le Soupçon le désert* (1978)
Y	*Yaël* (1967)
YE	*The Book of Questions: Yaël, Elya, Aely* (1983)

a b b r e v i a t i o n s

In the interest of simplicity and brevity, I have referred to Edmond Jabès's major works by abbreviation accompanied by page numbers, interpolated in the body of my text. When I have used existing translations, I have given first the reference to the English, then the reference to the original. All other translations are mine. Full publication data may be found in the Bibliography.

legibility

If I had to think of an ideal reader,
it would be the one who,
through my books, would take upon
himself his own contra-
dictions, his own dizziness, and would
learn, little by little,
not to fear them. In short, a way of
surviving. (DL 158)

The first question that Edmond Jabès's writing poses is the question of legibility. It is also the most urgent question, for all ulterior interrogations in that body of work, as well as any that I may raise in the present study, necessarily devolve upon it. Consequently, the approach to this question is of crucial importance. As a first step, it will be useful to render some of the theoretical problems entailed by the question of legibility more explicit. Why are Edmond Jabès's books so extraordinarily resistant to traditional strategies of reading? What are the specific conditions under which the Jabesian text may be read? What role does Jabès's work reserve for the reader and, eventually, the critic?

Initially at least, these problems and others contiguous to them are couched in a rhetoric of impossibility. This discourse derives from Jabès's sustained meditation upon writing and, more specifically, upon the "impossibility of writing, which paralyzes every writer" (BY 55, LY 59). Clearly, however, Jabès's attitude toward this impossibility is far from passive acceptance. On the contrary, he suggests that the writer must embrace the impossibility of writing, must recuperate it and remotivate it within the text as a functional, dynamic principle: "One must not hide behind the impossibility of writing in order only to write that impossibility; on the contrary, that illusory possibility must be pushed as far as impossibility; for nothing is written which has not been already rewritten many times over" (II 42).

There are certain moments in Edmond Jabès's work when writing turns back upon itself as if blocked and when inscription seems to encounter aporistic obstacles. The most obvious such case is in the discourse surrounding the Holocaust. Jabès faces a great dilemma: representation of the event here necessarily involves a troubling dimension of trivialization, yet to refuse representation is to refuse the significance of lived experience, as well as any lessons that history might have to offer.[1] The dilemma allows no compromise; Jabès's choice is to face it squarely, assuming its contradictions.

In a broader perspective, the way Jabès deals with the problems of writing about the Holocaust is figural of his poetics as a whole. That is, although most of the objects of his writing are of far less moral and historical import than the Holocaust, they nonetheless pose difficulties and contradictions as the writer grapples with them, which are consequent upon the *resistance* of any object (however banal) to writing, a resistance Jabès constantly iterates. As he develops this notion of impossibility, Jabès suggests that it is not confined to the writing act, but rather that the text inflicts its impossibility upon the reading act. This is part of a more ample field of speculation concerning the reciprocal affinities of writing and reading and the symmetrical relations pertaining between the two, a discourse I shall examine in more detail after having identified some of the specific conditions of legibility that Jabès postulates.

Here, however, he uses the notion of impossibility not merely to valorize his writerly activity and to suggest analogies between writing and reading (according privilege in this fashion to the reader's role) but also to protect his text from any threat of recuperation: "To put oneself back into question, for a writer, is to abstract one's book from any eventual attempt at appropriation by the reader, depriving the latter of the possibility of undertaking a global reading of the work" (DL 13). Impossibility arises in part at least from fragmentation and multiplication, processes which are inimical to any *possibility* of stable meaning. In describing the manner in which *Du désert au livre*, a series of conversations with Edmond Jabès, came about, Marcel Cohen notes certain problems, certain resistances:

We worked in this fashion for a while, before giving up once again: concerned about paralyzing the reading of his books, of which he had always said that their raison d'être was precisely to multiply possible readings without privileging any of them, even his own, feeling, like Mallarmé, "that there is no true meaning of a text," Edmond Jabès was not answering the questions. He was edging around them and neutralizing them so cleverly that they were no longer of any use at all. In fact, they demonstrated the impossibility of the initial project so clearly that they made one wonder why a stranger would intervene so persistently and awkwardly in a book by Edmond Jabès. (DL 10)

Jabès's canny strategy here is perfectly consonant with the one he projects in his books, where it constitutes an important element of his discourse of impossibility: "The book never actually surrenders" (YE 150, E 50). The consequences of such a strategy are far-reaching and may largely serve to explain the impossibility that recurs in the accounts of the Jabesian text offered by many critics.

Citing the incompatibility of the subject and the word in this body of writing, as well as its insistence on absence, rupture, and contradiction, Marcel Cohen suggests that Edmond Jabès's work cannot be penetrated by reading.[2] Sydney Lévy, alluding to much the same phenomenon, locates it in a problematic of impossible transmission:

> There is, then, in Edmond Jabès's books a kind of communicational impossibility. This is so not only because his questions remain unanswered, not only because his subject is dispersed, and not only because his words are overladen with meanings and therefore plural in signification. The impossibility exists also because the system he has built contradicts the very phenomenon that we call communication. In an ideal communication system, the object—as opposed to the sign—is absent from the transmission. There has to be a transformation—more precisely, a translation—of the object to be communicated into signals, which are in turn decoded by the receiver. In other words it is never the thoughts that are being transmitted but a translated version of them. In our reading of Edmond Jabès's books, we are getting something close to the object itself, and we are receiving it prior to translation, in the original version. His books do not tell us the story of something absent, but they show us plainly the very books that are being written. What is transmitted in his books is the book, and within that book another and still another, all three impossible, unfinished, unaccomplished.[3]

The impossibility that Jabès postulates for the writing act is thus, for many readers, effectively projected into the reading act. There Jabès will play with it to his distinct advantage, for an obstacle of this sort, once it is accepted by the reader, allows the writer to direct, and consequently *mediate*, the way the text is read. That is, the more the act of reading is bound up in enigma and obscurity, the more a reader may feel the need for certain specific hermeneutic instructions.

Clearly, then, the notion of impossibility is elaborated with considerable lucidity and care in the Jabesian text. Its projection on the writing and reading acts gives rise to other impossibilities. First is the idea of the *indicible*, the unsayable. Once again, Jabès seems to deploy this construct in an effort to subvert any possibility of conclusion or closure in the text: "The unsayable only haunts the accomplished sentence, the one which has gotten the best out of itself, as the unknown haunts us in our innermost self; that is, at the farthest point of being" (DL 72). The idea that Jabès wishes to elaborate through this discourse is that of a text that never *is*, but is always *becoming*, a text that consequently does not present itself as text, as static, finished artifact, but rather as writing, as dynamic process. Obviously, to the extent that Jabès succeeds in projecting such a vision of the text, it becomes more resistant to traditional strategies of reading: lacking any identifiable stability, the text becomes more difficult to apprehend.

Writing as process is consistently and radically opposed to speech in Edmond Jabès's work. In a most counterintuitive swerve, Jabès proclaims writing as the surest guarantor of unstable, polyvalent meaning, suggesting that writing functions to push the sayable beyond its limits. In this context, he evokes the notion of *exhaustion*: "Thus, writing, from one work to another, would be only the effort of the vocables to exhaust that which is said—the instant—in order to take refuge in the unsayable, which is not that which cannot be said, but rather, on the contrary, that which has been so intimately, so *totally* said that it no longer says anything apart from this intimacy, this unsayable totality" (PL 55–56). The proper mode of writing, then, is the unsayable; and its proper locus is a place (or, as Jabès would have it, a nonplace) situated beyond speech, a place where the common uses of words are no longer functional.

Writing becomes the object of a double displacement, a removal in both space and time: "The unsayable settles us in those desert regions which are the home of dead languages" (LB 77, EL 91). Jabès's location of writing is more precise than it might seem, and it is capitally important within his poetics. The association of writing with the desert, or rather the inscription of the former within the latter, is *crucial*, literally, in that writing and the desert are two transcendent metaphors in this body of work, which afford structure and coherence from one volume to the next. Jabès offers the desert as the radical other, a place of wandering and indeterminacy, a place defined, first, by its distanciation from places that are, or can be, known. Writing is to the desert as speech is to the known world, and Jabès postulates a stark dynamic of opposition between these sets of terms. The notion of temporal distanciation is analogous to the spatial: dead languages, after all, are precisely those languages that are no longer *spoken*, but rather *written* (and, significantly, *read*).

Apprehending the Jabesian text will be, then, to engage in a sort of archaeology. Any meaning is savantly bound up in layers of distance and deferral; if meaning is to be reached, it must be constructed through a patient teasing-out of that which Jabès offers as the unsayable: "In the unsayable, useless words lie hidden which we will claim later" (DG 49, LD 77). This is the reading contract that Jabès proposes, a contract in which the reader is unequivocally and unconditionally defined as a hermeneute, rather than as a mere repository of stable meaning. The contract clearly privileges the reader. Moreover, it is far more frank than those offered by most contemporary writing. It suggests that the reader will encounter problems which are very thorny indeed; nevertheless, those problems are outlined with lucidity and a certain precision.

The metaphor of reader as archaeologist is suggested by the Jabesian text insofar as it presents a vision of the book as an ancient artifact, an enigma to be deciphered: "Most of the time, a forbidden book" (YE 199, E 124). The reader's situation, on a first level, is analogous to that of Champollion. He or she must construct legibility from that which is apparently illegible; this process will involve painstaking work on the local level, a careful census of those elements in the text which seem to signify more readily than others. The reader will juxtapose and compare these elements, attempting to put them into mutual and coherent relation. In this fashion, a first (and very simple) reading grid can be established, a structure that may serve as a point of departure for other, more elaborate structures.

It is important to bear in mind, however, that Edmond Jabès's writing proclaims its resistance to any such process. Sometimes obliquely, but more often directly and frankly, this body of work advertises its hermetic character and strongly touts that hermeticism. Curiously enough, this problematic offers another point of *resemblance* between author and reader, for Jabès stresses that, if the book is enigmatic to its reader, it is equally enigmatic to its author: "Poring over the book, haven't I lived only in anticipation of the enigma's word which, although it is conveyed by every vocable, still to this day has never been deciphered?" (II 30). The insistent iteration of the concept of the text as enigma may help to explain why Jabès's critics, in their accounts of his writing, so often evoke the notion of alterity. When Joseph Guglielmi, for instance, suggests that Jabès's writing constitutes "an *unknown* type of discourse,"[4] he is reacting to the obstacles the text places in the way of traditional strategies of reading, the way it seems to block normative conduits of meaning and signification.

Henri Raczymow, one of Jabès's most perspicacious readers, has noted the tendency of critics to postulate this aporistic impasse in Jabès's work and to embrace it in order to clear away the need for interpretation.[5] Citing early critical reactions to Jabès's writing, Raczymow suggests that the enigmatic aspect of the Jabesian text was readily assumed and perpetuated in the accounts of the critics' encounters with that text—or as Raczymow would have it, in the lack of real encounter. He argues that most critics failed to engage Jabès's work in any but a most superficial manner, that they proclaimed before all else the "mystery" of this body of writing and fell back on reductive reading strategies wholly unsuited to his work. Principal among these, he notes, is the temptation of easy taxonomies. Thus Jabès was described in turn as a "Mediterranean writer" (like Char, like Camus); as a poet (but obviously and most importantly, as a "hermetic" poet); as a metaphysician; as a mystic; as a Jew. These labels, as different and unrelated as they may appear, share a crucial notion, that of *marginality*, defined, of course, in strict reference to mainstream literary tradition: Edmond Jabès's work evoked in many early critics the specter of the other. It was generally treated as an object of radical incomprehension, not to say dread. Through its refusal to come to terms with the special problems posed by the Jabesian text, criticism in these quarters abdicated its first responsibility. And ironically, it assumed precisely the problematic that it attempted to project upon the text: simply put, much early criticism of Jabès is *mystified* and, consequently, mystifying.

In this sense, allegations of illegibility may be seen to result largely from a refusal to interpret. For beyond the aporistic impasse described above, Jabès stresses that, for both writer and reader, the act of deciphering is vital. Moreover, as once again he accords privilege to process rather than product, Jabès suggests that the *process* of deciphering is precisely that which brings the book into being: "The book remains the enigma and the unflagging deciphering of the enigma" (SD 58). In a most roundabout manner, then, this is how Edmond Jabès guarantees the eventual legibility of his work.

In his view, interpretation is a most significant human activity, which implies a difficult but necessary assumption of liberty and accords a certain dignity to the person who undertakes it:

Interpretation is bound to act on the fate of individuals and of the world. It gives their destiny a new course, taking full responsibility for it, being ready to suffer the consequences and pay the price.

Also, interpreting the Book means first of all rising up against God to take voice and pen out of His power. We have to get rid of the divine within us in order to give God back to Himself and fully enjoy our freedom as men. (YE 146, E 44–45)

Jabès holds interpretation to be both a duty and a privilege. This is not to say that interpretation is an easy task or one that can be approached lightly. The person who would engage in it must necessarily confront a certain number of problems and avoid a certain number of pitfalls.

Jabès alludes very obliquely to one of these in the passage quoted above. Susan Handelman has formulated the problem more explicitly in an essay on Jabès and the rabbinic tradition.[6] Pointing out that the Jewish mystical tradition postulates the withdrawal of God, Handelman argues that this withdrawal causes interpretation to be open. (She says further that this is characteristic, if to a lesser degree, of normative Judaism as well.) For Jabès, she suggests, this opening is the very essence of writing and the locus of freedom for both writer and reader. Her point is well taken, especially in view of the highly idiosyncratic sense that Jabès attributes to the construct of "God" within his atheistic spirituality, his "Judaism after God."[7] The problem is that if interpretation is open, it is also ungrounded; that is, its very openness testifies that it has no reliable guarantor. Thus, though we are both obligated and privileged to interpret, and in doing so may affirm ourselves as independent beings, that act of interpretation will take place on terrain that is constantly shifting, and it will confront objects that are themselves unstable, nomadic: "Our lot is to interpret an unreadable world" (YE 84, Y 116).

Granted this openness, the notion of intentionality is far thornier in Edmond Jabès's work than in other bodies of writing. Nevertheless, any serious reader must come to terms with it on some level. As nonpertinent as any concern for authorial intent may seem to be in a poetics that proclaims the openness of interpretation to this degree, Jabès himself alludes to this problem. He foresees readings that deform his intentions and inserts them in a curious dialectic between reader and author: "You attribute things to me which are not in the book, things you think you have guessed. So I am baited by what it expresses against my will and by what you retain" (YE 248, A 59). Indeed, the dialogues that Jabès has engaged in with some of his readers, most notably Gabriel Bounoure, Marcel Cohen, Maurice Blanchot, and Jacques Derrida, as well as the traces of those dialogues in his published works,[8] suggest that Jabès views such an exchange not in a figurative sense but literally and that he has found a way to render it aesthetically effective.

Two other contiguous and related pitfalls should be mentioned. The first resides in a vision of the text as, before all else, a problem to be solved. The danger here is the reduction of the text, precisely, to its reading, a privileging of interpretive pyrotechnics over the object upon which they are exercised. The difficulty in achieving access to the Jabesian text, in this perspective, should not be considered as a savantly constructed *défi* to the hermeneute; it is, rather, significant (and significantly productive of meaning) in its own right. As Francis Wybrands has put it, "The obscurity of the text is not an obstacle to overcome; reading is not to triumph over the letter. Reading can only be defeat— confession and acknowledgement."[9] The second pitfall also involves a sin of reduction. It consists in regarding the text as a question awaiting an answer. Although it is always fatuous, I think, to approach a work of literature in this manner, the special characteristics—both formal and thematic—of Edmond Jabès's writing render such an approach particularly inefficient. Clearly, the question enjoys a special status in his work, and interrogation as a mode is used to deflect any possibility of sufficiency or closure before it can become established. The question is privileged, and the answer is consequently dismissed as having no place in this textual economy. Moreover, as Jabès notes once again the parallelism of writing and reading, he suggests that the structure of his writerly activity is analogous to the structure of any legitimate interpretive act that may be brought to bear on his work, insofar as both are dynamic processes of interrogation.

Edmond Jabès thus demonstrably assures the legibility of his writing. But, like other key notions in his work, he takes care to bind up the idea of legibility in a finely woven tissue of paradox and contradiction. This is what assails the reader on first approaching the problem of the specific conditions of legibility of these texts: on the literal level, the only assurance the author offers is that his work is "legible but illegible" (11 17). This paradox is frequently reiterated; it may be more elaborately formulated, but the essential, apparently irreconcilable contradiction remains, even when other terms are interpolated into it:

There is an invisibility that is deferred visibility, and a visibility that is discouraging illegibility.

This illegibility confirms to us that all that is visible is not, by virtue of this principle, legible, but that, on the other hand, that which is invisible remains the future stake of all legibility. (P 57)

Here, Jabès's game becomes more obvious, as he takes his primary pair of terms, legibility/illegibility, and puts them into play with another set, visibility/invisibility. He exploits the oppositional structure for its ludic potential, wagering especially on the symmetry of opposition. Moreover, the passage offers an example of a phenomenon far more rare in Jabès's work, for here he is plainly toying with graphic form. The preponderance of the letter *i* in the four terms suggests the visual act, the letter culminating in a point that graphically figures an eye. Other passages in Jabès confirm that he is attentive to the graphic form of the letter and of its possible efficacy in the text.[10]

Jabès's critics are quick to point out that his writing is illegible. Jacques Derrida, in his seminal essay on Jabès, alludes to the "radical illegibility" of *Le Livre des questions*;[11] he argues that this illegibility is neither irrational nor nonsensical, but rather one of the original conditions of possibility of the book itself. Joseph Guglielmi takes a similar position. Imitating Jabès's play with the paradox of legibility, Guglielmi speaks of the "illegibility of the legible," but goes on to assert that this illegibility is constitutive; it serves, that is, to construct the text. Postulating an agonistic dynamic of legibility and illegibility in the Jabesian text, Guglielmi suggests that this opposition accounts for much of the work's power: "*Le Livre des ressemblances* is the open battlefield of a conflict between the legible and the illegible."[12]

Jabès himself links this dynamic to a variety of other topoi. He specifically locates the notion of legibility in time, for instance: "The legibility—of the book—is related to the time—of the book" (II 19). Here, however, the apparent simplicity of Jabès's suggestion is considerably attenuated by the problematic status of time in his work: the Jabesian text is significantly and deliberately atemporal. He has, in a manner both cagey and playful, defined a groundless construct with one equally groundless; in so doing, he demonstrates most forcefully that legibility cannot be circumscribed. This is a technique that Jabès uses over and over again, in various guises. Elsewhere, for example, God serves as the guarantor of legibility: "The invisible form of the book is the legible body of God" (BY 231, RL 95). Later, he binds the paradoxical equivalence of legibility and illegibility into an adequation of divinity and unknowing: "The legibility and illegibility of God are the legibility and illegibility of nonlearning" (LR 134). But God, in this body of work, is the thorniest of notions. Jabès explicitly states that he invokes the term exclusively as metaphor (DL 87); its status as a signifier is thus highly unstable.

Similar problems arise when Jabès juxtaposes the problematic of legibility and the notion of mortality: "O death, in each word distinctly legible" (II 108). Here, legibility is attained only through death: " "Legibility is posthumous" (PL 24). Is this "death" that of the writer, of the reader, of the book, or of all three? For the book at least, the prospect of legibility is once again bound up in paradox and ambiguity. At times, for instance, Jabès postulates legibility as the death of the text: "In the book, then, life is but the passage from unreadable to readable and lost the very moment it is achieved" (DG 4, LD 12). Elsewhere, on the contrary, illegibility figures textual death: "The book dives and drowns in the books still to be written, which are only its repeated effort to escape death, that is, the unreadability to which it is pledged" (DG 37, LD 59).

It is clear in any case that Jabès's deliberate play with paradox here results from his own highly equivocal and idiosyncratic attitude toward legibility. On one hand, he speaks reverently about the cabalistic ideal of the perfectly readable book (DL 119); on the other, this perfect legibility, as admirable as he may find it in the abstract, is not an item on the agenda when his own writing is in question. On the contrary, he states emphatically that his writing must *resist* reading:

It would comfort me to feel that my books will continue to engender a certain uneasiness. I don't think that my books are "illegible." I don't think they are obscure. They become illegible only when one looks for certitude in them.

But perhaps you mean irrecuperable by "illegible." I do believe that their legibility resides in the fragment, but, as the fragments continually confront each other, the constitution of meaning is infinitely deferred. That is undoubtedly why they are irrecuperable.

Let's say, rather, that they should be such if one tries really to read them. But the fate of books, as you well know, slips away from their author. (DL 158)

Jabès's discourse here rejoins a capitally important figure in his work, that of the *margin*. Although that figure remains unvoiced in this passage, it is clear that other terms stand in for it. The Jabesian text is "irrecuperable": it is different from other texts, it is marginal. Its key integer is the "fragment": fragmentary writing proclaims its difference by its very form; its shape on the page advertises its marginal character. Thus the illegible comes to serve as a guarantor of marginality in Jabès's work: "In the margins of our pertinent readings, an illegible word remains a potential vocable" (LR 35).

What itinerary is available to one who would read Jabès's books, to one who wishes (as Jabès puts it so tantalizingly) "really to read them," *les lire vraiment*? It is important, I think, to remember Henri Raczymow's argument, and to put aside reductive approaches, reading grids that offer easy explanations of the author (as "Mediterranean," as "hermetic poet," as "mystic," as "Jew") or of the writing (as illustration of "humanism," "postmodernism," "deconstruction"). Sydney Lévy suggests a strategy that is most pertinent in this context: "Rather than reducing Jabès to a known paradigm, or rejecting him as incomprehensible, it is important to come to terms with his unreadability, to explore and exploit it, to move laterally on the surface of the text, tracing along meanings and resonances."[13] Reading Jabès must, then, be a very *local* activity. Just as the fragment centers attention on the corner of the page on which it is inscribed and seems to destroy any possibility of totalization before the latter presents itself, so reading must here be tentative, contingent on points of reference that are very dubiously grounded, under erasure, as it were.

Such a protocol of reading seems largely to conform to the various representations of reading that the text itself offers. Principal among these is the example of biblical reading, as Jabès suggests the analogy once again of book and Book: "The Hebrew people read the book of Moses like we would read a work given to us only in fragments" (LP 31). There are several salient characteristics of this reading act. First, it is fragmentary; the book cannot be apprehended in its totality but only in bits and pieces. Reading is thus necessarily disjointed and erratic. Moreover, Jabès seems to suggest that there are passages that will never be read, passages to which no reader can attain. These would constitute zones of mystery and taboo in the text; they would also serve to guarantee the text's marginality or, as Jabès puts it, its "irrecuperability." Finally, the reading act here is not a direct confrontation of reader and text but a highly mediated affair: some agency is parceling out the passages to be read. The text that eventually comes to the reader is selected and screened.

For Jabès, then, in one perspective at least, the distance between the reader and the text is considerable. The order of this distance is always double, as well, because it is both spatial and temporal: "Every reading is a reading of a foreign place, a first place" (LR 113). The proper locus of the book is both foreign and original, Jabès suggests. But it is important to note that these words function as deictics. They depend on a fixed point of reference which the passage does not voice. Clearly, however, that point is defined by the reader, or, more properly perhaps, by the locus of the reading. It is that locus that is "here" and "now." In a sense, the reading projects familiarity upon the text: it is a process of translation, even if only partial and fragmented. For Jabès argues that the reading will never quite "catch up" to the text: "You are always behind the reading of the book. It is the fruit of its own deciphering" (DG 79, LD 118). His remark can be interpreted in a couple of ways. Most simply, most literally, it is accurate to say that the first reader of any text is the author of that text. Consequently, any other reading is ulterior and supplementary in a sense. The other notion advanced in this passage is more problematical: Jabès here evokes the image of the text deciphering itself, effectively anticipating any interpretive act that may be brought to bear upon it. The vision of such a text rejoins Jabès's construct of constructs, the Book, a dynamic and largely self-sufficient entity wherein all possible literary modes and functions are conjoined. In this light, the book is *in process*, and always changing:

The book transforms itself as it writes itself. There would be, thus, different versions of a same text.
Which one are we reading? (P 9)

The protean character of the book is another guarantor of marginality. The fact that the text is not stable, and can never hope to be, erases any possibility of stable meaning. Reading must consequently be multiple because it reflects the multiplicity of its object.

Perhaps it is this consideration that leads Chiara Rebellato-Libondi to argue that any reading of Jabès must be a rereading:

The immense openness of Edmond Jabès's text, an openness constituted by the multiplicity of possible readings, the extreme freedom which is ours to multiply the latter still further, forces us to reread the word before and beyond its own deciphering.

One can read Jabès only by rereading him. One can approach his work only by erasing and redrawing the trails that his text points us toward, according to a proper system of mutations.[14]

Jabès is aware that the nature of his writing favors a multiplicity of readings, not only as idiosyncratic approaches differing from reader to reader but also (and most crucially) as any given reader will be led to accumulate a variety of different approaches to the text. The possibility of rereading offers the salvation of the text, Jabès suggests, in that it preserves and prolongs the text's dynamic character. Singular reading constricts and stabilizes and consequently does violence to the text: "Every reading limits. The unlimited text is the one which elicits, each time, a new reading, from which it partly escapes" (PL 83).

Thus it is clear that Jabès accords to the reader an extraordinary status. He demands uncommon attentiveness and lectoral responsibility but offers in return princely privilege. In the literary dynamic, the interplay of author, text, and reader, Jabès settles the principal importance upon the latter: "The reader alone is real" (BD 159). He sketches a detailed portrait of the implied reader of his work, insisting on positive qualities that will render reading possible: "A good reader is above all a sensitive, curious, exacting reader. In his reading, he follows his intuition" (DL 17). Of the four qualities he enumerates in this passage, Jabès returns most often to the notion of *intuition*. For him, this appears to be the key that finally allows entrance to his work. The implications of such an idea for his reader are singularly broad: on one hand, it constitutes a strong brief for lectoral freedom, for creativity on the part of the reader; on the other, it suggests that conscious choice and reason are not pertinent integers in this literary dynamic. The *real* reader of the Jabesian text (as opposed to the fictive construct that Jabès erects, the implied reader) is buffeted by problems and obstacles on every side as he or she attempts to comes to terms with this extremely difficult body of work. Marcel Cohen has suggested that reading Jabès is a *cataclysmic* experience that scars the reader. Recounting one's reading, writing on Jabès becomes for him thus a sort of exorcism: "It is to conjure up vertigo, to try and diagnose the illness in order not to face it."[15]

If anyone can be said to approach the status of ideal reader of the Jabesian text, that person is undoubtedly Gabriel Bounoure, one of Jabès's first and most faithful readers. In *Du désert au livre*, Jabès accords an extraordinary testimonial to Bounoure as critic, reader, and friend:

I was so intellectually confused that Bounoure was my last hope. Today, Bou-
noure has been forgotten, and I feel that this is an impardonable injustice.
The reading notes that he published in the Nouvelle Revue Française *and*
elsewhere testify to an unequaled critical acuity, as do his major essays,
collected in Marelles sur le parvis. *People saw him mainly as a critic*
concerned with the past. That's wrong: his last essays, devoted to René Char,
to Henri Michaux, and the letters that he wrote to young philosophers such as
Jacques Derrida prove on the contrary his extraordinary interest in moder-
nity.

He read the manuscript of Le Livre des questions *in 1962. He helped make*
that which frightened even me in those pages almost acceptable to me.
Further still, he showed me that my contradictions were the very substance of
my books, and that it was vain to try to avoid them. A long correspondence
followed. It helped me not only to assume my own chaotic experience, but to
deepen it.

Gabriel Bounoure's death in 1969, shortly before the publication of Elya, *which*
is dedicated to him, affected me most profoundly. Since then, I still feel that I
am writing under his gaze. (DL 81)

Jabès's work bears the traces of Bounoure's readings. His first essay on
Jabès was published in the *Nouvelle Revue Française* in February 1958;
it was reprinted as the preface to the first edition of *Je bâtis ma demeure*
(1959) and retained in the revised and supplemented edition of that
work (1975). His three essays on *Le Livre des questions*, published in
1965, 1966, and 1968, constitute a running commentary on that work
in progress, up to and including the fourth volume, *Yaël*. These readings are reflected summarily in the dedication of the next volume, *Elya*,
but more amply in *Le Livre de Yukel*, in which the protagonist-writer
addresses a letter "to Gabriel" (BY 131–34, LY 137–41).
In the preface to Bounoure's collected essays on Jabès, Gérard Macé
argues that Bounoure was more "reader" than "critic."[16] The nuance
here is important, I think. It emphasizes the primacy of the act (reading
presumably precedes criticism) as well as the dynamic process involved

in coming to terms with a text or a body of texts. For that was clearly Bounoure's great service to Jabès as he *read* each successive volume of *Le Livre des questions* in manuscript: his comments, suggestions, and encouragements were those of the *reader*. It is not overly surprising, then, that the reader's role should be so indelibly inscribed within the Jabesian text. Even taking into account the inevitable disparity between ideal reader and real reader, Jabès's writing suggests that every reader is privileged within the text, which reserves a significant role for him or her: "Every reader is the chosen one of a book" (LR 83).

The space that Jabès furnishes for the reader and the guarantees of eventual legibility that he offers are accompanied and supported by a set of explicit protocols of reading, the "directions for use," as it were, of the Jabesian text. These protocols are more or less precise. Sometimes they are alarmingly direct and unequivocal, as in a passage from *Le Soupçon le désert*: "My books ought to be read one after another, in the order in which they were written" (SD 9). Here, the narrative voice assumes an inhabitual authority over the reader, dictating an itinerary. Most of the instructions that Jabès proffers are more subtle and far more attenuated by contradiction and obscurity. "A book denounced by the book, it can only be read in the broken mirror of words" (YE 138, E 33) goes a passage in *Elya*; the image suggests, once again, that reading is necessarily fragmentary, reflecting the disjointed character of the text, of language, of words. The passage, however, occurs in a part of *Elya* entitled "The Broken Mirror of Words": the specularity of writing and of reading is thus underlined by the effect of *mise en abyme*. The mirror is a commonplace of modernist and postmodernist imagery,[17] and its function, like that of the language it often figures, is radically inadequate: the reflection it projects is deformed and nearly unrecognizable. The analogy that Jabès proposes thus implies that reading must deform its object, too; far from being a faithful and exact (re)presentation of the text, reading by the very nature of the act twists and transforms. Other instructions are similarly bound up in overdetermined metaphor, such that their hortatory function is largely obscured. "How can one read a page which has already burned, in a burning book, other than calling upon the memory of fire?" (LP 136), questions Jabès. The passage evokes holocaust both in general and in particular and seems to suggest that writing's catastrophic itinerary should be followed in reading.

Edmond Jabès recognizes, at least in his later work, that his writing poses special problems to the reader, problems not encountered in mainstream literature. He realizes that traditional strategies of reading will break down when brought to bear on his texts, leaving the reader feeling disarmed and helpless. Jabès suggests, however, that the act of reading itself reveals points of approach and ingress: "One enters into a book without being really prepared for it. As one proceeds with the reading, one takes responsibility for it" (P 40). The notion here is that the text constructs the reading, that, in this very different activity, one learns to do precisely by doing. Thus, on this point of his reading instructions, Jabès is frank and unwavering: "Reading is, perhaps, to persevere in one's reading" (LP 29). In iterating this point so insistently, he demonstrates incidentally that the irreducible intention animating all writing, no matter how apparently refractory to traditional approaches, is to be *read*; as obvious as it may seem to be, this point is capitally important in any discussion of the conditions of legibility of the Jabesian text.

Discussing specific procedures for constructing meaning in his work, Jabès returns to the notion of readerly intuition: "Don't hesitate, said Reb Garab, during your reading of the book, to note everything that strikes you in any fashion, even at the risk of making the ignorant laugh; for, behind the most obvious evidence that you find, a truth with incalculable consequences might well be hidden" (II 67). The situation presented in this passage is important and singularly illuminative of Jabès's strategy as a whole. The rabbi addressing his disciple is engaged in teaching the latter how to read. This dynamic in turn is a specular figure of the relation that Jabès proposes to his reader. That is, in a very real sense, Jabès offers to teach his reader how to read, commanding at some moments, coaxing gently at others: "In every book there is a zone of obscurity, a space of shadow that cannot be evaluated and that the reader discovers little by little. It irritates him, but he knows that therein lies the real book, around which the pages he is reading are organized. This unwritten book, both enigmatic and revealing, always slips away from the reader. Nonetheless, the intuition of it that the reader may have had is the only thing that allows him to confront the work in its real dimension; it's thanks to that intuition too that he can determine if the writer has in fact drawn near to, or on the contrary strayed from the book he aspired to write" (DL 119).

The idea that there is a book within the book, an immaterial text hidden from both writer and reader, is crucial in Jabès's work. Its implications are multiple. First, it tends to situate writer and reader isotopically, insofar as both are searching for the hidden text through their grappling with the material text (in the process of writing and reading, respectively). In addition, this cryptotext is a point at which real and ideal conjoin, a point of intersection of book and Book. Finally, it is a way around the problem of the radical inadequacy of language and a way of investing the nonlinguistic with significance and meaning. In the hidden book, Jabès argues, erasure and silence signify, too:

> To read in itself—and not only for itself—the book that one carefully deciphers.
> To read the erasure
> under the writing. (LP 32)

The rationale behind the fragmentary nature of the Jabesian text may be more apparent in this light. Jabès exercises all his considerable canniness here, suggesting to his reader that the text is composed of an agonistic interplay of the voiced and the unvoiced, of noise and silence. He calls upon the reader to consider not only what is written but also that which is *unwritten*: "To read this blank" (LP 73).

This invitation to throw oneself into the empty spaces of literature is, upon reflection, an extraordinary request to make of the reader. How else, though, can one approach the Jabesian page, structured as it obviously is on white emptiness and blank space? Or, as Jabès himself puts it, "How to read a story studded with blanks?" (LP 19). In an important early essay on Jabès, Maurice Blanchot addresses this question.[18] He argues that language is by its very nature fragmentary and that, moreover, the "interruption" that characterizes language is the function that allows us to distinguish the various elements of a linguistic discourse: "Interruption is necessary for any sequence of words. The gap makes becoming possible. Discontinuity assures continuity of understanding."[19] In this perspective, the blank spaces in literature assume a new, participatory role: they may be seen to be text rather than antitext. Jabès himself accepts Blanchot's analysis, agreeing that space is one of the necessary conditions of legibility: "You need space to read the world. Readability depends on distance" (BY 216, RL 79).

But I think that the status of emptiness in Edmond Jabès's writing is broader still than is suggested by Blanchot. In Jabès, the blank spaces do not merely facilitate signification, they actually *signify*. On a most obvious level, they point toward and rejoin the topos of emptiness, which is of primordial importance in Jabès's work. Moreover, in a formal sense, they structure the Jabesian page; the most characteristic, wholly idiosyncratic aspect of the latter is the gestalt it presents: a page from Jabès is instantly recognizable, and it resembles no other writer's page. Most pertinently, then, emptiness serves as a *signature* in this body of work.

Yet Jabès suggests that the role of empty space in his writing is even more ample. He intimates that the blankness should be *read*:

*One day, we will be able to read the white spaces between words
thanks to which we can approach the latter.*
God, on that day, will have lost the book definitively. (LP 15)

Clearly, for him, the blank spaces are not mere interstices. They may, rather, be the locus of the elusive construct to which Jabès frequently returns, the book within the book. Here, the legibility he speaks of is of a different order: the text he evokes is ideally transparent, like the book the cabalists dreamed of. Reading would entail a perfect totalization of meaning, an assumption of *all* that the text offers. Emptiness and silence would be decipherable and would constitute the highest order of the legible, for space would finally signify totally.

Once again, to demand such a reading seems, on the face of it, outlandish. This is all the more true in view of the special characteristics of the Jabesian text. For if that text often appears to be impenetrable, Jabès's exhortations to read the blank spaces point toward a place outside the boundaries of normative legibility. Yet his questioning here is undoubtedly genuine and is part of a broader interrogation. Jabès is calling upon his reader to motivate those textual elements which seem most refractory, to turn obstacles into operative integers. As the blank spaces figure distance and exile, Jabès suggests that they must be *read* into their opposite. The reader here assumes extraordinary status in the literary dynamic, but the last role he or she is called upon to play is more important still. For the most problematic space that Jabès alludes to is the distance between the writer and the text, a distance that the reader is asked to repair: "There is an impassable space between writer and book which the reader is called on to fill" (YE 25, Y 36).

This image announces the final level of Jabès's discourse on reading and legibility. Here, he suggests the essential similarity of the activities that the writer and the reader engage in. Their status is thus analogous; they confront largely comparable obstacles and fall into the same traps: "Writer and reader lose themselves in the same vocables" (DD 95). The implications of such functional parallelism are far-reaching. Speaking of the readers of classical Hebrew texts, Jabès suggests that the absence of diacritical marks forces the reader to greater attentiveness, that he or she must jump from comprehension to intuition to recreate the word: "It's at this point that the reader rejoins the creator who, as he penetrates into the writing, acquires the intuition of the book. Thus there is not one book in the book, but innumerable books" (DL 118). Creative reading in this perspective *becomes* creation.

This is the crucial clause in the extraordinarily rich textual contract that

Jabès proposes to his reader. He encourages the reader to engage fully in textual production, iterating constantly that writing finds its double in reading, even if the reader is unaware of that, "for every reader, at the most intense moment of reading, is also an unsuspecting creator" (II 69). He states explicitly that the order of this creative act is precisely analogous to that of the writer and that active, creative reading entails a very real appropriation of the book: "Every reader is a potential writer. He makes the book his book" (P 88). Jabès's vision here is similar to that of Roland Barthes, who called for a reevaluation of the reader as *producer* of textuality.[20] In this light, reading is an imperative, a creative obligation that Jabès calls upon his reader to assume:

However, does reading the book not mean creating it by and by? Taking the book on yourself to such a point, does this not mean being born with and of it? Does it not mean being bound to make your own book, that of your spirit, of your soul and your body? Otherwise, reading would only be intellectual curiosity.

Reading a book in this way, adopting it in its fullness, means substituting another book for it—identical, it is true, yet so marked by the particular, often original approach that it modifies the first. Because every true reader is a potential creator, and writing, at this degree of penetrating a text, means only reading what is quietly writing itself within your reading.[21]

Beneath the appearance of impenetrability in this writing, then, a surprising contract awaits the reader: Jabès offers a full partnership in the enterprise of textuality. He assures us that the seeming illegibility of his work is a surface phenomenon and that persistent approach to the text will render it legible, that reading in fact is possible, even if the necessary and highly desirable end of reading is to put itself, along with its conditions of possibility, radically into question:

That which outside is illegible is, inside, legible.
The writer strains tenaciously to make the outside inside, and the inside outside.
Writing might be only conspicuous glimpses of possibility. (DD 34)

Q..

the letter

To each book,
its twenty-six letters;
to each letter,
its thousands of books.

(PLS 19)

Polished, symmetrical, and forbiddingly hermetic, Edmond Jabès's work defies its readers to find ingress. In each text, Jabès erects obstacles to parry traditional reading strategies; moreover, his work explicitly questions its own legibility. But as Rosmarie Waldrop has pointed out, paradox is one of the principal motors of this literary machine.[1] Thus as the reader seeks to deploy ever more arcane means for unraveling the textual knots, he or she may neglect other, simpler strategies. One of these, I think, is as productive as any other in approaching Jabès's work. It is based on a *literal* reading; that is, a reading devolving initially upon the individual, precombinatory letter. As reductive as such an approach may at first appear, one of its principal merits is that it is suggested by the Jabesian text itself, which proposes the letter as the generative locus for a series of crucial problematics, among the most consistently salient in Jabès's work: writing, absence, and death. With its congruent topoi, the letter serves as the counter-term in the paradox of reading, subverting the affirmations of radical illegibility and guaranteeing the underpinnings of the legible: "The labyrinth is simple in the yet simpler letter" (BY 203, RL 69).

Through the mediation of the narrator-scriptor in *Elya*, Jabès characterizes himself as a "man of the Letter" (YE 132, E 23); elsewhere, he speaks of a "thought devoted to writing . . . which recognizes the primacy of the Letter, which makes it the basis of His contemporaneousness" (YE 294–95, A 121). In this, Jabès rejoins certain medieval traditions (which will be examined presently) and participates in a current of postmodernist literary experimentalism also exemplified by the work of Georges Perec, the Oulipo, John Barth, and Walter Abish.[2] In 1964, Jacques Derrida noted Jabès's insistence upon the letter and located it at the base of his literary project, at that time still very much in its formative stage.[3] Other critics have voiced much the same argument. Agnès Chalier, for instance, states, "Jabès's poetic act is effectuated in the erasure and the surging forth of the letter."[4] Gabriel Bounoure, one of Jabès's first critics, and considered by the author as his ideal reader, also recognizes the primal character of the letter in Jabès and attributes to it a recuperative function, suggesting that the letter can somehow repair literature: "These days, writing is all too frequently foully debased, but the letter (whose function is to destroy the effect of time) rediscovers, traced by the poet, its original character. Reinvested with their antique power, the symbols of the word and the graphic sign obey their metaphorical essence, that is, their transpositional vocation."[5] Joseph Guglielmi argues the absolute priority of the letter in relation to the word, suggesting that Jabès favors the letter in reaction against the apparent unicity, the seeming totalization implicit in the word: "The imperious mobilization of the letter in the course of its conflict with the word (or, if one prefers, the confrontation of phoneme and morpheme, installing a new order of meaning) becomes, not without contradictions, the cardinal moment of the Jabesian project. In other words, it is the promotion of the letter as motor of the production of meaning and at the same time as propagator of the unknown and exemption of meaning. It is the placing *outside of meaning* of the word identified with the void where, like turbulent, modulated, dancing letters, the *fragments of a world to be recreated* tumble about."[6]

Though these critics and others have remarked upon the importance of the letter in Jabès's work, they have not pursued the problem much further than that. In this chapter, in a manner both interrogative and citational, I will trace the problematic of the letter as it winds through these texts, to follow it like the Ariadne's thread it may prove to be. For I suspect that Jabès proposes the letter as a sort of *mode d'emploi*, encouraging his readers to use this tool in their efforts to build coherence, to make meaning.

In the analysis of the status of the letter in Jabès's work, temporal considerations predominate. Jabès characterizes the letter as an ancient artifact, perhaps the most ancient of all artifacts. Indeed, in a curious and counterintuitive swerve, he postulates that the letter preceded the word: "The letter is the grandmother of the word" (LB 64, EL 74). This notion participates in the larger struggle between the letter and the word to which Joseph Guglielmi alluded; but the reasons for this conflict, and its consequences as well, may be broader than they seem. For, as Jabès argues the anteriority of the letter, it becomes clear that his argument favors the graphic at the expense of the phonic: Jabès is not principally interested in speaking, but rather in *writing*. Under this circumstance, the precedence of the letter, the minimal graphic sign, over the word may appear more plausible.

As he states the chronological priority of the letter, Jabès erects as a corollary the logical priority of the letter in a series of entities culminating in the Book: "So with each letter in the word, with each word in the sentence, the Book begins" (YE 282, A 103). The model proposed here is that of the pyramid, a structure broadly based on the letter in its material aspect. Moreover, this notion seems to be a constant in Jabès's work; indeed, a text from *Je bâtis ma demeure* presents a rigorously analogous model, interpolating other terms:

The letter steals the word which steals the image which steals.

The letter lies to the word which lies to the sentence which lies to the author who lies.

The letter dreams the word which dreams the sentence which fulfills the word which fulfills the letter.

The letter unbinds the word which unbinds the image which unbinds the day.

The sentence adorns the word which adorns the letter which adorns absence.

The letter spends the word which spends the sentence which spends the book which spends the writer who is ruined. (BD 301)

Often, Jabès locates this series within the Judaic tradition, sometimes through suggestion, sometimes explicitly and categorically: "I repeat: The sign is Jewish./ The word is Jewish./ The book is Jewish" (YE 290, A 114). As Derrida pointed out, Jabès draws an equivalence between the Jew and the poet;[7] the letter may thus be seen to figure the initial and irreducible sign of poetic activity. Derrida, however, defines the poet as "the man of speech and writing": the conjunction of the two activities and their rhetorical order are misleading, at least in Jabès's case. For speech in Jabès is wholly ancillary to writing—the former activity assumes an incidental status—and the letter must be considered iconically to subsume written language.

The series that Jabès evokes, whose most frequently recurrent elements are the letter, the word, the sentence, and the book, are clearly hierarchies. Moreover, each step in the hierarchical structure is effected through a combinatory process, as letters combine to make words, words combine to make sentences, and so forth. The letter, then, serves as the minimal but nonetheless authoritative integer in this process. Again, Jabès's insistence on this point reflects certain trends in postmodernist literature; Georges Perec's view of the literary text as a combinatory system, for example, is similarly based on the letter: "It still astonishes you that the combination of thirty-odd typographical signs, according to rules which are after all very simple, be capable of creating, every day, these thousands of messages."[8]

Other, more venerable traditions are also reflected in this aspect of Jabès's poetics, most strikingly perhaps the theories of a thirteenth-century cabalist named Abraham Abulafia, who elaborated a system called *Hokmath ha-Tseruf*, or "the science of the combination of letters."[9] Therein, letters and their configuration are used to achieve a mystical state through meditation; Abulafia likened it to "a music of pure thought," the alphabet supplanting the musical scale. As Abulafia's combinatorics result in contemplation of the divine, so Jabès's result in the Book, that highly personalized construct whose multiple attributes approximate the divine. This constant linking of word and book according to a combinatory process in Jabès seems intuitively plausible in a linear sense; but, strangely, Jabès points toward the reversibility of the process, as the aggregate dissolves into its constituent parts: "Later, we saw the book as nothing more than the letters of each of its words, and watched this alphabet, infinitely repeated in different order, slip through our fingers like grains of sand" (SD 7). This statement tends to reinforce still further the congruence of the letter and the book, to such a degree that, in some instances, they may appear to be indistinguishable: "We write not with letters, but with exhumed books" (P 30). Jabès sees in Hebraic letters the universalized form of the book (P 29), as if each individual integer were a product of, and a repository for, thousands of its homologues: as book supplants letter, so letter supplants book.

This speculation rejoins another tradition of occult theories of the alphabet, according to which each letter of any given alphabet embodies a set of mysteries proper to it alone.[10] More important for our purposes, it points toward another aspect of the letter as Jabès defines it. Not only is the letter postulated as a graphic sign, a two-dimensional entity, it comes to assume still more materiality, entailing volume and extension in space. As the letters become concrete, as they occupy space, even the space separating them begins to play a role; indeed, at one point, Jabès locates truth in this interliteral space, if provisionally and in a conditional, interrogative mode: "Then where is truth but in the burning space between one letter and the next?" (YE 7, Y 13). The notion is largely analogous to one expressed by Maurice Blanchot in an essay on Jabès's work, wherein he argues that discontinuity (or the empty spaces in a text, whether actual or figural) serves, precisely, as the guarantor of understanding.[11] In the combinatory process, the newly assumed materiality of the letters is transmitted to the words they eventually come to form: "The word carries the weight of each of its letters" (BQ 26, LQ 26).[12] In this manner, progressively, the immaterial, ephemeral oral sign is banished from the hierarchy as Jabès, much like Derrida, continues to expand his brief for the graphic, according privilege and, more crucially, *authority* to writing at the expense of speaking.[13] Gabriel Bounoure argues that one function of this strategy entails, paradoxically, a revalorization of orality, that the graphic sign "saves" the oral by its very visibility.[14] This may well be the case, but it would seem to be more a happy coincidence than the principal consequence of the process; the intent, rather, is to arrive at a redefinition of writing itself, based on the letter. Jabès's short meditation on the letter *I* illustrates this point nicely:

"The letter I," he said, "this vertical line with its two tiny horizontal serifs, is a straw in the mouth of emptiness which blows so limpid a bubble that only a momentary reflection of the light can betray its presence.

"A point like a head cut off its body and become soul again in its fleeting, soapy roundness, only to burst on contact with space.

"Writing is the childhood of the void, an exorcism of the letter, of the word." (LB 64, EL 74)

Visibility, verticality: Bounoure sees in this aspect of the letter a "stasis of affirmation," likening it to a pyramid culminating in the invisible.[15]

Equally significant is the attribution of human characteristics to the letter, a course of progressive personification that constitutes the next step in Jabès's strategy. "I let ink run into the body of every letter I guessed, so that it should live and die of its own sap" (BQ 36, LQ 37), says he, evoking homunculus myths from Pygmalion to Frankenstein. Among these myths, however, one seems to resonate more strongly than the others in Jabès's work: the myth of the Golem.

Gershom Scholem describes the Golem as a manifestation of letter magic, a myth resulting from belief in the incantational power of the letter: "The creation of the Golem was, as it were, a particularly sublime experience felt by the mystic who became absorbed in the mysteries of the alphabetic combinations described in the 'Book of Creation.'"[16] According to certain versions of the legend, the Golem was a clay statue that was brought to life by the inscription of five letters upon its forehead; were one of the letters to be erased, the Golem would return to dust. Its function was to protect the community; in times of crisis, it would rise up and save its people.

The parallels between this myth and Jabès's poetic enterprise as a whole are striking: as the letter animates the Golem, so it does Jabesian *écriture*. That *écriture*, moreover, like any experimental writing, explicitly proposes new modes to the literary community, new possibilities of salvation in a sense. In this case, those possibilities are grounded in a combinatorics of the letter, a belief in its aesthetic efficacy that verges on the mystical.

The process of personification continues as the letter appropriates the name: "One letter dropped from your name, and already you are no more" (YE 245, A 55), says Jabès, echoing both the Golem legend and another tradition according to which a Torah transcribed by hand is deemed useless if one of its letters has been lost or deformed in the transcription.[17] Even the *scream*, the one essential, transcendent sound in the Jabesian text, originating in Sarah's madness, perpetuated in the septology by Yaël, Elya, and other voices, continuing to keen through the later works, becomes a letter composing the name of the person voicing it (YE 185, E 102). The letter, given the mediation of the name, defines and embodies identity: perhaps in counterpoint to Rimbaud's famous dictum, Jabès arrogates the *je* to himself, noting that it is composed of his own initials (DG 1, LD 9). He also associates himself with one letter above all others, typically refusing to identify and thus demythify it: "One letter among all the others is my true home. Each time I find it in a word, sometimes twice or three times, I tremble with happiness" (LR 14).

If this statement clearly rejoins Jabès's characterization of himself as a "man of the Letter," some critics detect a broader concern in his insistence on the letter, an inscription of the cultural history of Judaism. Edith Dahan, for example, materializes this concept in arguing that circumcision constitutes a literal marking, a branding of the letter in the body, concluding that "the Jew is the victim of a violence of literality."[18] Although that argument is never categorically stated in Jabès's works, his personification of the letter, through the name, does entail a corporeal fusion in which the letter transubstantially incorporates the person: "Participating in the formation of the name, it creates, through the latter, our image. It ceases to be anonymous then, and becomes one with us. It embraces our condition or our incondition, lives and dies with our life and our death" (DL 18). As the letter evolves, the amplitude of its function increases; no longer a semiotic artifact bound up in a necessarily deforming web of representation, no longer confined to mere taxonomic status, the letter begins to *be* and, in being, it guarantees the existence of that which it incorporates: "Four letters sufficed for God to be God" (DL 18). With this enunciation, the final stage in Jabès's elevation of the letter is attained: from the human, it accedes to the divine.

In this accession, the reader encounters one of the principal nodes of paradox in Jabès's works. For, even as he insistently evokes the divine, Jabès proclaims his atheism. Actually, his stance engenders a great deal of aesthetic efficacy, particularly since his discourse, from the early works to the present, has been based so firmly in the interrogative mode: in the divine, as traditionally conceived, resides the answer, the totalizing affirmative, the anathema of the Jabesian text. Still, like the Temple and the Tablets of Law (irretrievably lost and thus unattainable), the divine is a source of considerable longing in Jabès. His work strains toward it, while amassing the evidence of its absence. This practice is crucial in defining Jabès's notion of a "Judaism after God" insofar as it is only through this straining toward a nonexistent end that the possibility of value appears.[19]

The letter leads Jabès to defer God. Drawing a distinction between *Dieu* with a capital *D* and the concept of divinity, Jabès suggests that his denial and the poetics of absence resulting from it are directed toward the former, rather than the latter (DL 106). He takes pains to point out, moreover, that, though he frequently uses the word *Dieu* in his discourse, it is to be taken in a metaphorical sense, like the word *juif.* He even goes so far as to identify the tenor of the metaphors, God representing the "void" and Jew the "torment of God, of the void" (DL 87).

Again, his tactics are fraught with paradox, and deliberately so: metaphor is, after all, a transcendent linguistic figure insofar as it engages complex semiotic orders. To deploy it explicitly and consistently in a discourse that presents itself as atranscendental results necessarily in paradox. But, as Jabès proceeds to the deification of the letter, this paradox motivates his text: "God spoke, and what He said became our symbols. The shape of a letter is perhaps the shape of His face. God has as many faces as there are letters in an alphabet" (LB 62, EL 72). Just as the letter, in its concrete form, figured the book, so now it figures the face of God, encapsulating in this manner the taboo of representation. For if the Judaic tradition proscribes the visual representation of God, so the Jabesian text swerves away from conventional representation, increasingly so, from the *Livre des questions* to the *Livre des ressemblances* to the more recent works. The main concerns of this body of work—death, loss, absence, emptiness, silence—defy visual representation and, in a broader sense, are extraordinarily resistant to other representational modes. The letter, then, supplants these modes and serves as a cipher for the unsayable, that discourse which cannot be voiced: "God's silence has the dimensions of the Letter" (YE 265, A 80).

As it plays this role, the letter participates in a function which Jabès, elsewhere, rigorously excludes from his work: transcendence. If he argues that God is "the unquenched desire of the letter" (YE 334, A 171), that argument must be interpreted in the context of the full range of metaliterary discourse in these texts. Seemingly, with regard to Jabès's own literary enterprise, the letter oversteps even those limits erected by the text. The transcendental function is accompanied at this final level by another, which, in other contexts, Jabès is equally quick to denounce: totalizing: "A sole letter can contain the book, the universe" (CS 59). If his rejection of the apparent totalizing power of the word was what initially led Jabès to turn to the letter, if he for similar reasons rejects the notion of God, he nonetheless attributes this surpassing, irreducible power to the letter such that, even as the letter serves as the base of the combinatory pyramid discussed earlier, it also ciphers the invisible with which that pyramid is crowned.

The problem of guaranteeing the structure remains. In most of the mythology surrounding the origins of language, God serves as the guarantor. But as Gabriel Bounoure points out, if God has absconded, the letter is no longer grounded, no longer adequate: it becomes void of significance.[20] Jabès himself plays on this notion at some length, juxtaposing mutually exclusive possibilities, exploiting the resonance of contradiction. Again, he expresses the contradiction in literal terms: "As with God, the letters which designate us scatter and yet stay with us" (LB 103, EL 121). In the final analysis, however, Jabès, deferring logic, relies on practice, attempting to prove motion, as it were, by walking: that which serves (provisionally and contingently at least) to guarantee the letter is the text it produces.

"One letter in common is enough for two words to know each other" (LB 10, EL 15): upon this terse confession of faith devolves a major aspect of Jabès's poetics. Adopting the letter as his point of departure, he exploits it in a mode of meditation best characterized as analogical, using it to erect *resemblances* throughout the hierarchy he proposes. Beginning on the level of the word, this process of analogy will serve as an agent of coherence in texts. Eventually, it will help to unify bodies of texts, including the seven-volume *Livre des questions*. The first step in this process is to juxtapose individual words, to establish correspondences based on the letter:

He said: "Justice and Loi, *'Law,' have one vowel in common. This letter is their only link. It is also found in the word* Bien, *'Good.'*
*"*Mal, *'Evil,' shares a consonant with* Loi. *Both Good and Evil ripen in the shadow of the Law. But Justice only sides with Good."*
He also said: "God is not good. He is good writing." (YE 205, A 9)

There is a certain will toward reconciliation at work here, testifying again to Jabès's belief that the letter can somehow be exploited to repair language. And, in certain examples, a ludic impulse is also apparent: "Deprived of the air of its *r*, *la mort*, 'death,' dies asphyxiated in the word, *le mot*" (LB 33, EL 39). Here, obviously, Jabès is playing on words or (more appropriately) on letters; the game depends largely on its graphic aspect for its effect, which derives from the transubstantiation of the letter. As letter becomes word, Jabès reaffirms his contention that "every letter is a name" (YE 283, A 105). Yet this game is colored by the sobriety of the tone in which it is announced. Moreover, the two words juxtaposed are far from innocent playthings; rather, they are two of the most overdetermined words in Jabès's lexicon, and they enter the game fully armed with all the rhetorical consequences they have acquired in the septology. The notion of the ludic aspect of Jabès's poetics of the letter will have to be reexamined after consideration of examples that are more intricate on the combinatory level. For the moment, suffice it to say that Jabès insists on the determinative power of the individual letter through word to text. He argues this point vigorously in an epistolary text addressed to Jacques Derrida, suggesting that, in one notable case at least, Derrida has deployed a literal strategy similar to Jabès's own:

You are against all forms of repression. First and foremost, there where the book solicits you, you are against the repression exercised upon the letter; for the letter is, perhaps, an origin diverted from the origin, granted that it is bound to a signified whose weight it must in part support.

It is thus that in the word différence, *one letter, the seventh, was exchanged against the first letter of the alphabet, in secret, silently. And that sufficed for the text to be other.* (CS 58)

On the next level, Jabès turns to letters in combination, drawing words together, forging correspondences on the basis of a plurality of common letters. Although most of the pairs or series or words he evokes are not mutually anagrammatic in the strict sense (since some of their letters vary), Jabès's speculation in this area is clearly anagrammatic in nature. It exploits the principal attraction of the anagram, that trembling of sense which occurs when words considered to be very different (because of the dissimilarity of their semantic fields) are shown, *literally*, to be alike. The strangeness of the anagram, its shock value, undoubtedly derives from its aleatory character: whereas we intuitively attribute motivation to semantic convergence, we feel in most cases (etymological linking being an exception) that literal convergence is based on chance. Jabès recognizes this and plays on it, but his real intent, I think, is to recuperate the aleatory, to demonstrate the higher motivation offered by the letter and, eventually, the text. Considering the word *soif*, he muses:

I have watched fall and, falling, come apart the letter "s," then the three others. Then I thought I could read in the mirror of the void, where they had in passing looked at themselves, the word foi.

Foi, *faith in the book. Faith in the letter.* (YE 334, A 171)

Similarly, Jabès speculates upon the word *amour*, noting its resemblance to *mort* (BQ 141, LQ 55) and *mur* (LB 47, EL 56); other examples abound in Jabès's work.[21] In all of them, however, the semantic correspondences are called up and put into play only after the literal correspondences have been evoked, as if the former resulted from the latter. In this manner, Jabès reverses the hierarchical relation of the literal and the semantic, according privilege and (perhaps more important) priority to the literal.

Robert Duncan associates this aspect of Jabès's writing with Ferdinand de Saussure's work on anagrams.[22] Other similarities may, I think, be noted. Like Jabès, Saussure abstracts the letter from the text; refusing to consider it as merely a nonsignificant combinatory integer in the system, he uses it to erect other systems. But there the paths of the two diverge, for the valorization of the letter effected by Saussure is only temporary, as the letter again assumes the status of nonsignificant integer in the higher-order combinatory system it creates, whereas in Jabès the letter retains its priority, serving as figure both of origin *and* end. Perhaps more closely affinitive is one of the cabalistic techniques of mystical speculation, *Notarikon*, in which the individual letters of a given word are interpreted as abbreviations of whole sentences, thus in some measure retaining their priority.[23]

Gabriel Bounoure sees in Jabès's letter play an echo of surrealist praxis, arguing that he evokes "the erotic intercourse of the letters, of the consonants and the vowels, to allow words to make love, as André Breton put it."[24] He thus adopts and amplifies Jabès's personification of the letter, pointing toward its generative power. Joseph Guglielmi locates Jabès's anagrammatic speculation at the foundation of his poetic enterprise, suggesting that it is actually a process of destruction designed to liberate words from the discursive, enabling them to accede to the poetic: "The only thing that counts is the *literal* work, which uproots the word . . . from its secular ground, and casts it upon the unknown paths of exile and desert."[25]

If examples of this practice run throughout Jabès's work, there is one text that seems particularly influenced by it, wherein the *resemblance* of two words accounts for the genesis of writing and continues to nourish the text as it proceeds. *Récit* is a meditation upon the words *il* and *île*, upon their similarities at first and, progressively, upon their differences: masculinity and femininity, subject and object, writing and written. As the text oscillates between the two words and between analogy and contrast, the writing process appears as more clearly dialectic than in other texts, a dialectic based on the letter and stripped of all *fioritures* that are not literally pertinent. The oscillation may be compared to another aspect of Abraham Abulafia's science of the combination of letters. According to Gershom Scholem, Abulafia advocated *dillug* and *kefitsah* in his method, or "jumping" from conception to conception.[26] Scholem suggests that this is akin to the technique of free association in psychoanalysis and to certain techniques of surrealism. This "jumping," argues Scholem, "brings to light hidden processes of the mind" in both psychoanalysis and surrealism. If one accepts that the intent of both is to reveal that which is normally overlooked, to elaborate, through appeal to the elemental, a new and more viable structure, the intent of *Récit* appears to be very similar. A minimal text, terse and dense, *Récit* may be taken as a manual of Jabès's poetics of the letter, where the "story" ironically announced in the title demands, in a very real sense, a literal reading.

Another cabalistic tradition based on the letter seems to resound in Jabès's play on strict anagrams: *Temurah* is a method of mystical speculation contingent on the "interchange of letters according to certain systematic rules."[27] It is, like "jumping," a means of acceding to a higher state of consciousness. This impulse bears witness to a nostalgia for transcendence, reveals a will to (as Jabès anagrammatically puts it) *"Nier le Rien* [To Deny Nothingness]" (P 105).

A special case of the anagram, its most perfected form, is presented by the palindrome. It figures prominently in the last volume of the septology, as Jabès superposes the word *nul* on the word *l'un*, the former made of black dots on a white background, the latter of white dots on black (LB 52–53, EL 63). The physical presentation is important for several reasons. First, the pointillism of the inscription recalls the point that serves as the title of the text and immediately engages the whole problematic of the point and the discourse that Jabès erects upon it. Second, it reifies the specular relation inherent in any palindrome, which entails mutual reflection according to a mode that is, paradoxically, both faithful and unfaithful to the object. In this manner, through this image of letters, Jabès proposes an important *point*, arguing the reciprocity of words. Georges Auclair convincingly reads Jabès's palindrome in the light of cabalistic theories of the sacred character of language: "When Jabès enunciates the palindrome *L'Un* = *Nul*, isn't he, as an atheist, inviting us to see that French also holds secrets (troubling thought) that only a patient or inspired search for hidden permutations of letters within words can reveal?"[28] If vestiges of a fictive but nonetheless much regretted original language resonate in the palindrome, Jabès seems to suggest that the symmetry and purity of original language can be recaptured in some measure through painstaking work on the letter.

The anagram assumes special importance in the septology, where the names of the principal characters (or, more precisely perhaps, the *voices*) in the fourth, fifth, and sixth volumes are Yaël, Elya, and Aely, respectively: these names are, of course, mutually anagrammatic. Adolfo Fernandez Zoïla speaks of Yaël's "formative letters," suggesting that she creates the other two in a literal manner.[29] His argument is all the more persuasive since the characters in the septology become progressively less corporeal and more ethereal: Yaël is already less fleshed out than Sarah and Yukel, who dominate the first three volumes; Elya, her stillborn child, speaks from beyond death; Aely is the disincarnate *regard* of everything and nothing;[30] El is the point, wholly lacking spatial extension. The letters, then, are formative in that they afford these voices some materiality, some tenuous being. The notion that Yaël literally generates the others in the series is proposed by Jabès himself:

Oh Yaël, your name, broken at the far end of silence, was restored in death. But who was it that took such poor care of it?

Its letters got scrambled by accident, and an unfamiliar name, "ELYA," was
formed on the sand where it had been a long time since anybody had expected
anybody. (YE 125, E 13–14)

In similar fashion, Jabès traces Aely's origin to the sign: "It is through
signs that Aely compelled recognition. . . . Imagine my surprise to find
an alphabet there traced in stone" (YE 332, A 168).

Jean Frémon sees in these names "a combinatorics which will shortly
become invested with a hidden meaning, inaugurating a series whose
norms, echoes, and similarities will be impossible to determine, the
trace of a common origin, an indefinable family resemblance."[31] They
are names and also titles of texts. They afford coherence and a degree of
unicity to the voices they designate, and their function with regard to
the texts is analogous. Moreover, on this metaliterary level, they point
toward a significant aspect of the Jabesian text. Each successive work
may be read as a combinatory exercise upon preceding works, as
familiar elements are transposed, inverted, woven into the fabric of the
new text in a striking pattern of autoallusion: gloss upon gloss, writing
upon writing. In this sense, the anagram is figural of Jabès's broader
textual strategy and goes a long way toward explaining his predilection
for grouping his texts in series, his will to make them mutually cohere.

These anagrams evoke yet another consideration. Composed of four
letters each, they are tetragrams recalling, for a multiplicity of reasons,
the Tetragrammaton, the unpronounceable name of God. In written
Hebrew, the vowels of *Elohim* or *Adonai* are interpolated in the letters
of the Tetragrammaton; modern transliteration in the Roman alphabet
results in several variant forms, the most common of which is *Yahweh*.
The anagrams in the septology demonstrate a progression away from
this word: the first syllable of *Yaël* reproduces the first syllable of the
name of God; in *Elya* this syllable remains intact but is deferred; in *Aely*
its component letters are split, and the sound is not voiced; in the
point, *El*, it is absent. In Jabès, as we have seen, the letter is often
proposed as a figure of a divinity who has absconded; thus the ana-

grammatic series in the septology can be seen to recapitulate the "story of dead letters in their four letters" (LR 95).

Jabès's literal combinatorics again demonstrate certain affinities to those of Abraham Abulafia, which Scholem describes as follows: "Basing himself upon the abstract and non-corporeal nature of script, he develops a theory of the mystical contemplation of letters and their configurations, as the constituents of God's name. For this is the real and, if I may say so, the particularly Jewish object of mystical contemplation: The Name of God, which is something absolute, because it reflects the hidden meaning and totality of existence; the Name through which everything else acquires its meaning and which yet to the human mind has no concrete, particular meaning of its own."[32] In Jabès's work, granted his atheism, the reconstruction of the name is doubly impossible; yet his writing is a discourse on the impossible, and it yearns toward the name even as it embraces the absence the name has left behind.

Before returning to the Tetragrammaton, whose importance in Jabès is far broader than I have thus far suggested, I should like briefly to discuss certain other examples of letter play and the status that Jabès accords to them. In the final volume of the septology, he raises the ante in the game of word convergence on several occasions, devoting full pages to the graphic juxtaposition of the anagrammatic series already discussed, to the words *livre, libre, lire, le,* and to the words *dieu* and *deuil* (LB 38, 70, and 73, respectively; EL 45, 81, and 85, respectively), disposing the letters on the page such that the *resemblance* of the words they form is unmistakably apparent. One such example is particularly pertinent:

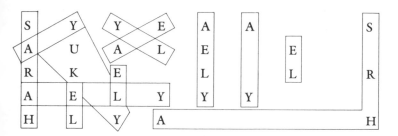

(LB 57, EL 68)

Visually, this graphic image resembles a crossword puzzle, another word game based on literal convergence and intersection. In the crossword puzzle, as Georges Perec (an accomplished cruciverbist as well as writer) has pointed out, priority is attributed to the letters as they fill the grid; the semantic aspect, the elaboration of the definitions, follows upon the former.[33] This, of course, is highly consonant with Jabès's own practice. The image can also be regarded as a table, a table of contents in fact, recapitulating the septology as a whole. In this way Jabès clearly encourages the reader to regard the septology as an intersective work, a labor of correspondences and resemblances. Just as obviously, he suggests in this manner that the structure of the septology depends on the letter: therein, as Jabès graphically demonstrates, the letter is *crucial*.

Other examples of letter play include the acrostic and the abecedary; in these, as elsewhere, the ludic aspect is considerably attenuated by the sober tone of the discourse and (in one case at least) the nature of the subject. For the most part, Jabès's work refuses temporal and spatial location, but in one of the relatively rare instances when he directly and unequivocally engages current political debate, he does so with vigor. In a short but uncompromising text written for the antiapartheid movement, Jabès denounces the South African regime; his text includes an acrostic exercise on the word *apartheid* (DD 45–47). Again, the import of the subject addressed and the passion of the author's tone tend to subvert the ludic element characteristic of the acrostic as a form.

Jabès's abecedary constitutes an inversion of the norm: it catalogs proper names from Zacharie to Adrien (YE 328–29, A 162–64). This is itself significant, reflecting a multiplicity of other inversions in Jabès. More significant is a lacuna in the abecedary, which slips from "Kui-Yuan" to "Ismaël" (in reverse alphabetical order, of course), omitting the *J*. This omission may be interpreted in a number of ways. The absent *J* may recall Jabès's own name; it reflects the erasure of the *je*, the subject, to which he alludes elsewhere in his work. It may be considered as a circumscription of the Judaic theme and the void, which, as Jabès stated, it metaphorically represents; in this case, his strategy—inscription by omission—would seem particularly well chosen. Or it may figure the absent divinity, the *J* being the transliterated *Yod* of the Tetragrammaton, the *J* of Jehovah. Such interpretations are mutually complementary. Still, the remark with which Jabès closes the passage would seem to privilege the first of them: "Alphabet book, as old as its worn letters and different inks, I see my name disintegrate and reform in it any moment" (YE 329, A 164).

Regarding all his letter play, Jabès's position is both curious and intransigent: "Actually, nothing is farther removed from traditional word play than the use that I sometimes make of it" (DL 133). Acknowledging the experiments of James Joyce and William Burroughs in this domain, he suggests that in his case the early influence of Max Jacob was more important (DL 135–37), yet he recounts how Jacob progressively and beneficially discouraged his attempt to imitate the former's verbal alchemy: "He taught me to be myself, that is, *different*" (DL 28). Jabès insists categorically that he does not "play" with orthography in his texts (DL 129); in qualifying the literal experiments in other bodies of work as "dangerous games" (DL 134), several questions arise. Why are these games dangerous? Who or what do they threaten? How do Jabès's experiments with the letter differ from those of other writers? Tentative, elliptical responses to these questions may perhaps be found in a further examination of the role of the Tetragrammaton in Jabès's work.

"The four letters JUIF which designate my origin are your four fingers" (BQ 19, LQ 18), says one of the voices in the *Livre des questions*. The notion of origin, like that of the center, is extraordinarily problematic in this body of work; it is in turn dislocated, denied, and deferred, yet it remains the object of constant longing. The passage identifies the four letters as those composing the word *juif*. Elsewhere, however, Jabès argues that *that* tetragram merely serves to figure, if imperfectly and provisionally, the Tetragrammaton in its absence (SD 57–58). Jabès explicitly associates the Tetragrammaton with writing: "A man of writing is a man of the four letters which form the unpronounceable Name" (YE 250, A 60). The implications of this association are complex and startling, for in effect it constitutes a firm location of the Tetragrammaton as both origin and center of writing: origin because the inscription of the divine name serves as the first example of writing, the divinity as first writer; center because, according to Jabès, it continues to inform and control any act of writing: "Thus any page of writing is fashioned under the sign of four letters which are the masters of its fate, with power to make it disappear through the expedient of the words containing them" (YE 250, A 61).

The contradiction seemingly inherent in this strategy is one in appearance only, however. Far from materializing the ineffable under the influence of the materiality and presence of the text, the power of the Tetragrammaton is such that it achieves the dislocation of the text into the realm of the ineffable and the absent: "Writing of silence, letters of chalk" (YE 296, A 122).[34] Again, even within the minimal combinatory structure of the Tetragrammaton, each individual letter retains its authority because each individual entity reproduces the phenomenon described by the whole, ontogeny, in a sense, recapitulating phylogeny. Thus the erasure the Tetragrammaton causes is reproduced in the "four erased letters of His name" (YE 216, A 23); in similar fashion, the silence that the name decrees is, clearly, a *literal* silence: "Four times God fell silent in His Name" (LB 97, EL 113).

The Tetragrammaton unifies letter and number. Jabès himself speaks of the relation of the number four to the infinite (LB 99, EL 115); elsewhere, he suggests that the letter and the number are united in the process of writing: "The resemblance of the letter and the figure, of the vocable and the number, resides in the equivalence of their respective value of use and exchange. We count when we write, said Reb Cherki" (LR 107).[35] Guy-Félix Duportail argues that there is an "algebra" at work in Jabès's writing and likens it to the *Gematria* of the cabalists, a mystical technique Gershom Scholem defines as "the calculation of the numerical value of Hebrew words and the search for connections with other words or phrases of equal value," the numerical value of the words deriving from that of the letters composing them.[36] Jabès works toward the unification of the letter and the number in the latter part of the septology. "O sameness of the letter and figure in the heart of the final sign" (YE 333, A 169): this sign is the point which serves as the title of the "last book." Neither letter nor number, it *resembles* both, the last sign remaining before signs are erased.

Erasure, absence, silence: Jabès bases his writing on these topoi, normally anathema to the literary text. As he describes it, they emanate from the Tetragrammaton as it exercises its sway over the text: "All writing embraces, finally, the unpronounceability of the name of Yahweh" (LR 140). In the context of literature, granted Jabès's valorization of the written at the expense of the oral, the unpronounceable results in the unwritable. As Jabès inscribes the Tetragrammaton in his texts, its multiple manifestations are characterized by a striking degree of orthographical variance. Jabès writes both "J.H.W.H." and "Y.H.W.H." (A 114; LR 105), "Yahvé" and "Yahveh" (LR 140; II 22), "Je suis Celui qui est" and "Je suis Celui qui suis" (EL 93; LD 91). This variance in Jabès's work is not trivial, but on the contrary highly significant. It may be viewed in the light of a passage in which Jabès recounts childhood memories:

As far back as I can remember, and insofar as I can be certain, I think it was my childhood spelling errors that were the starting point of a questioning that has grown in importance since then. I couldn't understand why a word written a little differently, with one letter too few or too many, should suddenly cease to represent anything at all; that my teacher should angrily cross it out in red ink in my notebook, and allow himself to punish me for having, as it were, invented it.

A word existed, then, only if it were written correctly, or as someone—but who? God, perhaps?—had chosen, ordained, that it be written. Unless that which was called "use" was nothing other than a conspiracy of letters? And how had these letters acquired so much power over people, in order to impose themselves in this manner? What mystery was hidden in them? Sometimes I thought that, in spelling a word my way, I might live alone with it, be the only one to love it. (One can only invent words of love.) I dreamed, in an outburst of brotherly love, of a new language for a secret society. I felt, among my disputed vocables, both free and a slave to their freedom. (SD 57)

The difficult, disappointing lesson was undoubtedly (demonstrably in fact) learned: to be read, one must obey certain orthographical rules. And indeed Jabès is capable of eloquent argument in favor of these rules, as he warns of the dangers of orthographical experimentation in the literary text. But again there transpierces a nostalgia for the "victory" of the child over language, society, and environment as that child performs a personal, original act in writing a first word (DL 128–29). Writing has lost that original power, Jabès seems to suggest, both in his own practice and historically, yet that power is the end toward which any writing must strain. Testifying to this, Jabès adopts the Tetragrammaton, exploiting both its transcendence and its indeterminacy, and erects it as a figure of writing. In doing so, he claims and retains the right to *write* it in any way he sees fit, coercing meaning to adhere to the various letters he chooses. This process in the microcosm is largely transferred to the macrocosm, given the former's exemplary status: it serves as an important tool in Jabès's ongoing efforts to repair the literary text.

The role of the Tetragrammaton in Jabès's work is analogous to that of the other aspects of his poetics of the letter discussed here, even as the Tetragrammaton largely subsumes them. In the elaboration of this discourse a series of paradoxes is deployed; all, to varying degrees, resist resolution, but one among them seems to be irretrievable. An imaginary rabbi enunciates one of its terms: "The work of writing would be, then, the reiterated affirmation of the adherence of the letter to a specific place" (LR 113); he sees this place as the reunion of all places, Eden and the Promised Land, origin and end. But in a long iterative litany, another rabbi argues that we are unable to create because we are unable to repeat the literal combinatorics that account for the original act of creation: "'If we cannot create the celestial canopy,' said Reb Josua, 'it is because we do not know the mysterious arrangements of letters with which the heavens and the earth were conceived'" (LR 44). Divine origin of language is continually deferred and thus cannot serve the text, in the final analysis, as a source of salvation. Similarly, Jabès annuls the possibilities offered by the human origin of language, bound up as they are in the contradictions of representation: "In frustration, man invented the sign, which, at first, was merely the image of an image, the representation of an irrepresent-able in search of itself" (P 25).

The alpha is thus obscured and unattainable and so is the omega: "I enter the neatly sectioned world of the alphabet with the few letters which recall me. What a distance between the will to be and the wording of this will" (BY 56–57, LY 61). Language remains inadequate, insufficient to the needs of expression; clearly, for Jabès, the letter is at the nexus of this dilemma. It is the wandering sign of all wandering signs, pulling everything it constructs into exile and dislocation, a figure, through the literary text, of the human condition. In continually frustrated but nonetheless ever-renewed expectation, the letter, like the text it engenders, awaits an impossible resolution: "A twenty-seventh letter remains perhaps to be invented" (LB 22, EL 27).

the word

To each word,
its share of ink.

(BD 302)

Among contemporary writers, Edmond Jabès is distinguished by the extraordinary attention he devotes to writing, to its modes and elements. Postulating a combinatory hierarchy, a pyramid whose stages are defined by the alphabetical letter, the word, the story, and the book, he scrupulously guarantees that each stage receives its share of ink. A significant part of this process devolves upon a persistent, rigorous interrogation of the lexicon; as deployed within the Jabesian text, it results in a sustained meditation on words and their uses.

Adolfo Fernandez Zoïla has noted this questioning of the word and has argued its importance in Jabès's aesthetic: "Jabès has been carried away by words; their profound tropisms, their consonances have dictated their expression, their associations, their erectile transformations into sentences."[1] Gabriel Bounoure has suggested that a mythology of words is apparent in Jabès's writing.[2] On several occasions Jabès himself has confirmed these critical insights. Like Stéphane Mallarmé, Jabès is strikingly obsessed by the impossible ideal of the Book, and he favors one book particularly: "The dictionary is one of the books on my bedside table. I dive into the *Littré* or the *Robert* each time I find a moment to spare. The life of words amazes me. For me, their death is almost a source of grief" (DL 73).

The frequent occurrence of rare and archaic words is perhaps the most immediately apparent feature of Jabès's idiolect. Marcel Cohen, noting examples such as *malemort*, *défets*, *acaule*, *détisé*, and *solacier*, argues that they are indicative of an attempt by Jabès to swim against the current of linguistic drift, to strive toward the purity of original language (DL 72). In response, Jabès remarks that words such as these offer a passage into the forgotten, a means of partially recuperating the past. Changing terms, he characterizes the effect of the injection of archaic words into an otherwise normative discourse as a sort of *dépaysement*. They contribute to the abolition of regular notions of time in the literary text (a concern that is progressively more obvious in Jabès's writings as, from *Le Livre des questions* onward, they become ever less narrative and consequently less located in time). The stark intrusion of the past contributes to the creation of modernity, as any modernity must necessarily oppose some anterior model (DL 72–74).

Further, for most readers, the referential status of these words is largely erased; in consequence, words appear initially as just ink. Having survived their connotations and denotations, the archaisms are singularly notative: they demand to be read, simply and precisely, as *words*, as opaque entities whose place in the textual economy is justified by their very materiality. Thus each functions, according to its degree of opacity, as a sign of Jabès's broader discourse on the poetics of the word. Eventually, they connote anew.

Edmond Jabès's writing is also marked by certain obsessional words, certain key words that recur with regularity. "There is, in the text," says Jabès, "something imperceptible which haunts us; a key word which obsesses us" (P 91). In this manner, he alerts the reader and whets the curiosity of the hermeneute. Elsewhere, he elaborates this notion further, offering examples from the septology:

Who could still deny that, under certain obsessional words—in Le Livre des questions, *the words "God," "Jew," "Law," "Eye," "Name," "Book": God, as extreme Name of the abyss. Jew, as figure of exile, of wandering, of strangeness, and of separation; a condition which is also that of the writer. Book, as impossibility of the book or, rather, as both place and non-place of any possibility of the edification of the book. Eye which is the Law: "In the word* OEIL, *there is the word* LOI. *Every gaze contains the Law." Name, as unpronounceability of the Name, as annulation of all names, silent Name of God, of the invisible—who could still dispute that in certain words of our intimate vocabulary (as if transparently), a story that is probably more truthful than the one which we pride ourselves on living is writing itself little by little?* (SD 85)

Calling attention to recurrent words makes them even more conspicuous. The autoallusive inscription of the septology within the trilogy and, moreover, the fact that these words continue to insist in the text tend to draw Jabès's writings together in a synchronous whole; they serve to erect intertextual *resemblances* among Jabès's various works, pushing his books in the aggregate toward the Mallarmean, totalizing ideal. These words, then, are intended to transcend the limits of the book, to take their place in the Book, as both its components and figures. Jabès's technique in this passage is that of the lexicographer. As he elaborates his dictionary of obsessional words, he implies that in one of its aspects at least, the Book will be precisely that: a dictionary.

Other words might well be added: *dwelling, desert, sand, void, margin, scream*. Still others, even more frequent and connotatively charged, Jabès uses, exploiting the poetic potential of tautology, to denote words themselves: *mot, parole, verbe,* and (especially) *vocable*. As with the archaisms, the principal role of these obsessional words is firmly situated on the level of metacommentary, as Jabès unremittingly puts writing and its norms into question. The obsession with the word and the obsession with the Book are thus mutually dependent, for each iteration of these words constitutes a specular emblazoning of writing within text and consequently of Book with book.³ In an elegant analysis of one of these words, Pierre Missac has argued that *margin* may be offered as a key to the Jabesian text, suggesting a reading which is not based on the metaphor of ingress but on a notion of circumspection.⁴ Explicitly directing his reader's attention toward certain key words, Jabès takes pains to suggest that any doors they eventually open may lead nowhere: "The key word opens not upon the word, but upon the void" (11 30). In like manner, but from a different perspective, he adumbrates the inadequacy of the key word as a hermeneutic tool, since it remains beyond the grasp of the reader who might wish to use it: "A priori doubtful, interpretation of the book, because, at every turn, it is challenged by the opaque light of some word that might well be the key" (DG 3, LD 11).

Deliberately enveloped in paradox (of which the oxymoron *opaque light* is a model in miniature), Jabès offers and simultaneously retracts his obsessional words. Affirmation, negation, and, once again, tautology: the words that resound most provocatively in these remarks about key words belong to that order, respectively, *void* and *vocable*. One is left with the image of a dictionary in which the definition of any given word is merely an iteration of that word.

Throughout this work, Jabès furnishes commentaries on the word *vocable*, glosses as it were, which serve cumulatively as a rather precise redefinition. One of the most interesting of these occurs in his conversations with Marcel Cohen: "Thus the word 'vocable' which, since Mallarmé, had been almost entirely neglected by writers; only linguists continued to use it. Given its new environment, this word assumes in my books, I think, unlooked-for colorations, transgressing its etymological meaning, often bordering on neologism" (DL 73). First and most obviously, Jabès considers *vocable* to be an archaism. Its function is analogous to that of other archaisms in his work: a verbal evocation of the past and a partial recuperation of memory, a certain exoticism and effect of *dépaysement*, creation of modernity through contrast to an anterior model. His allusion to Mallarmé is highly significant. Mallarmé, a poet of the word, a writer of the Book, is one of Jabès's principal literary touchstones. Further, Jabès implies that part of the process of re-motivation may involve the extraction of a word from its normative context (the discourse of linguistics) and its situation in a new context (the literary text). Through the use of the metaphor *colorations* he suggests the materiality of the word *vocable*. His final remark is very curious indeed: transgression of etymological meaning approaching neologism. Here, he implies relations that would seem to be aporistic: is *vocable* a case of the old in the new or the new in the old?

Clearly, Jabès is aware of the etymology of *vocable*; elsewhere in his work, he points out that it derives from the Latin *vocare*, to call (SD 95). Any transgression of etymological meaning may be very venial. Sydney Lévy has argued persuasively that the etymological roots of *vocable* account for much of that word's force in the Jabesian text.[5] According to him, the most heavily charged words in Jabès's lexicon "call" to each other along a multiplicity of different axes; the example he offers, that of *seuil* (threshold) and *seul* (alone), functions by orthographic and phonetic analogy. Mutual attraction affords tension to the text (Lévy invokes the metaphor of vibration to characterize this), as words continually strain toward one another. Moreover, the "call" that *vocable* inscribes on the page may be read as the call of God for the Jew, the call of the Book for the writer. In Jabès, Lévy suggests, the meaning of exile is "exile from the call in order to be *what* is called." Thus the voicelessness of the *vocable* and indeed the entire mode of writing which it figures, like Sarah's cry in *Le Livre des questions*, exemplifies and eloquently testifies to the helplessness of ink.

Joseph Guglielmi contrasts *vocable* to *verb*, saying that Jabès prefers the former because it is more neutral, less solidly grounded in religious tradition and the notion of origin.[6] Still, in one of his glosses on that word, Jabès links *vocable* explicitly to religious tradition: "To abolish the graven image as the second commandment orders, to reject representation in order to stress the transparency of the word [*vocable*]: seen and yet indistinguishable, heard and yet inaudible" (YE 188, E 107). What he is suggesting is very similar to the evacuation of reference in the archaism, liberating the word from its burden of representation, although here Jabès plays with the notion that the end product of such an evacuation is a material object, subjecting that notion to the warp of paradox, characteristically shying away from any fixed teleological result. More important still, Jabès here reveals himself as an iconoclast, remorselessly breaking his own idols. His first implication, that the real is ineffable, is a commonplace subsumed by a further implication, a moral proscription: the real is forbidden. For Jabès, the idolatry of the word is the guiding dilemma of language and writing.

In spite of these remarks, the materiality of *vocable* in Jabès's work strikes the reader. Agnès Chalier, for example, states: "The theatricality of the word is expressed in the materiality of the 'vocable.'"[7] Jabès himself must surely be aware of the materialistic connotations of *vocable* as it is used in linguistics. Even the dictionary (which does not designate the word as archaic) insists on the material quality of *vocable*, which is defined as a syntactic rather than a semantic artifact, a word considered as a grouping of orthographic or phonetic integers rather than as a unit of meaning.

As Jabès continues to gloss *vocable*, as he continues to redefine and overdetermine the word, he pushes his distinction still further, moving away from the abstract toward the concrete. In one instance of this

strategy, he contrasts *vocable* to *mot*: "One can *say* a word; one can only read a vocable. Would the vocable then be the written word?" (LR 86). A rarity among the many questions posed in Edmond Jabès's work, this one seems to be purely rhetorical. Clearly, for him, *vocable* is the written word of all written words. The evacuation of the phonetic aspect results in a purely orthographical artifact, voiceless sign of writing and figure thus of the Book. Moreover, further comparison of *mot* and *vocable* suggests the relative position of each in the hierarchy of obsessional words. "The very last word stands just before the first vocable" (P 56), says Jabès, once again arguing that speech must lead to writing and, implicitly, that writing as human activity must claim ascendancy over speech. The word in Jabès is thus subject to a *devenir*; its status is that of a *becoming* rather than a *being*. It becomes *vocable* as it is incorporated into the Book, in which it assumes a referential status, first connotatively and, progressively, denotatively, as each occurrence of *vocable* in Jabès's discourse comes to serve as a signature of *écriture*.
This becoming, however, would seem far too linear: first, strip the word of all referential and representational function; then, evacuate its phonetic aspect; finally, inject it and remotivate it within the written text. But Jabès distrusts any sort of linearity. He is quick to subvert the notion of the end, to defy any finality with paradox and indeterminacy. In the very act of according privilege to *vocable*, locating it at the top of a hierarchy, he subjects it to this general rule, showing that it, too, results in aporia: "The word [*vocable*] always faces the unknown" (YE 332, A 168). Thus this most heavily laden word, this most determinate word, is suddenly and unequivocally plunged into indeterminacy. The progression closely resembles a process of ritual sacrifice, the deliberate offering up of a privileged being, *vocable* as fatted calf, vestal, or firstborn son: "The words [*vocables*] have disemboweled the words" (BY 79, LY 85). Confirming this impression is another passage in which Jabès speaks of the *vocable* as prey to the void: "Here I have to stress how strongly the word [*vocable*] is attracted to the nothingness around it for which it is the preferred prey" (YE 161, E 68).

61 ❖ The Word

The extraordinary instability of the word *vocable*, reflecting the inadequacy of the entire lexicon, exemplifies and largely accounts for the broader (and perhaps more troubling) instability of reference in Jabès's writings.[8] This is all the more true insofar as, for Jabès, words precede things and beings: "The fact is that, in order to exist, one must be named. Nomination precedes us. So it was this nomination that I tried to discover first of all; a nomination which is merely the realization of that which is or will be; which preceded then the thing, and which will conquer the universe" (DL 121). Here again is apparent a nostalgia for the original. The initial act of *nomination* which Jabès wishes to recuperate through imitation is clearly bound up in the notion of the divine; to engage in such a project is to attribute to oneself some sort of divinity, however modest.

Assuming for the moment that words precede things and granted the unequivocal manner in which Jabès valorizes written language over spoken, the book is the only possible crucible for this experiment in recuperation. As he regards his chances of recreating the real, Jabès's tone is at times remarkably sanguine:

I wanted to say that, in the book, things—beings as well, inevitably—evolve in a universe of vocables: their universe. Thus, the world is in the book. Perception of the universe is mediated by words, and we quickly realize that this perception is nothing other than our metamorphosis, at first unconscious, then recognized and accepted, into a word. We become the word which affords reality to the thing, the being. To write is to measure oneself continually against this reality, in order to embrace it. Finally, everything is real, and it is in this perspective that we ourselves are real. (DL 128)

Following this current in Jabès's thought, one detects a certain trust in the process of writing as a means of repairing language, as a means of securing the relations of the subject and surrounding phenomena. All of this is predicated on the materiality of the written word: "To make the word visible, that is, black" (BD 155). The attribution of materiality through writing underlies Jabès's argument about the precedence of words over things and may account for his curious leap of faith. This leap involves a counterintuitive swerve: just as he reverses the typical hierarchy in which we arrange the written and the spoken, so he operates on words and the phenomena they denote. By extension, his argument applies to the book and the reality surrounding it: whereas we might normally consider a book to be a representational artifact, a more or less complex semiotic system framed in relation to the real, Jabès argues that it is only within the book that one can have any hope of creating, precisely, the real.

On the level of the word, such an argument entails a process through which normative denotation is put sharply into question, sidestepped or deliberately neglected. The word assumes materiality in the written text; the objectivity of the thing to which it normally refers becomes secondary to the acquired objectivity of the word itself. This may help to explain Jabès's fascination with neologization: each new meaning that he proposes to any given word serves to attenuate that word's normative representational function, which he sees as hopelessly compromised. Using the metaphor of the moth and the flame (and, in passing, that of Baudelaire's albatross), Jabès characterizes this process of remotivation of the lexicon as a fight for survival: "Around a word, as around a lamp. Powerless to leave it behind, doomed, insect, to be burned. Never for an idea, but for a word. The idea nails the poet to the ground, crucifies the poet by his wings. In order to live, other meanings of the word must be found, a thousand must be offered for it, the strangest, most audacious, so that its fires, dazzled, cease to be deadly. And there are unceasing flights and dizzying falls, leading to exhaustion" (BD 156). The prospect of recreation, the will to repair fallen language, allows Jabès to pursue his enterprise even as he contemplates the abyss of signification. Georges Auclair has recognized this tendency and has argued that, though Jabès is demonstrably tormented by the rift between words and things, that rift stimulates and nourishes his writing.[9]

Conflict is continually inscribed on the page in a clash of metaphor: "We will make every word [*vocable*] into an impregnable fortress with determined stones" (YE 135, E 28); "In this closed universe, every word [*vocable*]—even while I form it—becomes a lock in which I turn the key. Imprisoned, I no longer know where to knock" (YE 282, A 104). The formal parallelism of the two passages is striking. Both are dominated by the overdetermined word *vocable* and both, through the adjective *every*, insist on the singularity of the work of writing at the level of the word. Both, moreover, exemplify what I have termed the *devenir* of the word, the process of becoming as it assumes materiality and objectivity. But a formal parallelism is sharply undercut by the apparently antithetical relation of the metaphors. Fortress and prison, both are imposing structures, both enclose the subject, but they imply radically different relations between the subject and the world. The former guarantees the subject's security and survival in a hostile world, the subject moving within in an effort to escape that hostility; the latter, on the contrary, concentrates hostility within, while the subject vainly contemplates the security of the outside world.

Such paradox is highly illustrative of Jabès's most troublesome dilemma. As he labors to erect his dwelling, his *demeure*, he is at once king and prisoner, both creator and the object of annihilation. In some sense, then, a dwelling, or a book for that matter, must be fortress and prison simultaneously in view of the seemingly irreparable schism in the verbal sign. Perhaps poetry amplifies the equivocal function of language, rather than repairing it.[10] Perhaps, in Edmond Jabès's writing at any rate, the functional principle is one of dissonance, as words and things, straining toward each other, continually fail to coincide harmoniously: "The word surprises the object, dawn the night. Hence object and word reflect one another as do sky and earth by the hour. The word pulls the object out of its limitation; the object wants to be the reason and the sense of the word's adventure. The word lets us see and hear the object; the object gives its share of light and dark to the word. The object and the word which designates it take part in one and the same separation. The space they try to cross is the threshold which keeps them apart. Hope of joining prompts them to brave the void; but this nothingness, the home of promises, is it not death?" (BY 155, RL 17). Jabès thus launches the problematic of words and things, like the meaning of *vocable*, into the void. And the dissonance in his language, grounded in loss, is figural of death. Creation and annihilation are mutually implicative in Jabès's work, as each act of inscription implies an act of erasure, as *littérature* implies *rature*.

If each word, as Jabès suggests, "initiates a mortal existence" (BY 173, RL 37), this very mortality testifies to its anthropomorphic character. For words and human beings are insistently identified in Jabès's writing. Both, as individuals, live and die; they share, as members of their respective orders, a history and a future: "The weight of words is undoubtedly nothing other than the weight of man's experience; the weight of a common past and that of the intuition of a shared future" (DD 80). Adolfo Fernandez Zoïla has argued that this identification of word and person is the principal mark of Jabès's *œuvre*, calling the latter "a relativizing machine, a repeated attempt to unite word and man."[11]

Jabès describes his relation to words as isotopical, a dialogue among equals:

I have for a long time been on good terms with words. But this does not mean that they always show a liking for me.

Some mornings I have endless trouble tackling them. Everything irritates them. We face each other like dog and cat. I am the dog, of course. My faithfulness is sorely tested lying in wait for the moment of transformation when the cat turns dog to please me. (YE 15, Y 23)

The locus of identification is displaced into a neutral ground, that of the animal: man as dog, word as cat. One metamorphosis clears the way for another, precisely that which is most crucial to Jabès's writing, which *allows* him to write: in pleasurable, ludic interchange, word becomes man, man becomes word.

The process of personification recurs frequently in Jabès; this, too, of course, is part of the *devenir* of the word. Each door is guarded by a verbal keeper (BD 155); words seek each other with the sad look of separated lovers (BD 302). Words wander through the Diaspora of the Jabesian text; their wanderings imitate those of the Jew, of the writer, of the author himself.[12] Writing can be characterized as a ritual of seduction: "The writer's art consists in persuading words, little by little, to take an interest in books" (BD 174); "Difficulty of becoming part of the word and sharing its fate" (BY 56, LY 60). The resulting text contains the verbal inscription of the sexual act: "I write to you with the flesh of rushing, panting, red words" (BD 204). Gabriel Bounoure has argued that words, like letters, are sexual beings who obey a "superior erotic"; the poet affords them conjunction in the text.[13]

But sexual reciprocity is colored in Jabès by a certain aggression: words hold the poet within their dominion. They are both strange and familiar, constraining and resisting the poet as he struggles to integrate them in the text, sometimes saving the poet, sometimes condemning him to death: "Words which are foreign to man, comfortably installed in our memories, words which banish us, tyrants. And it is also a word which saves us. And it is always for one of them that we commit suicide" (BD 155–56). As the notion of fictional character (that is, the adequate representation of real human beings) is progressively erased in Jabès's work, as characters from Sarah and Yukel onward become progressively more disincarnate, the word comes in some fashion to fill the vacuum left behind.

Through the process of personification, the *vocable* in a sense becomes an actant in the text, a human or humanlike being participating actively and decisively in that aspect of the Jabesian discourse which to such a large degree affords it its originality and aesthetic force, the questioning: "I owe my uneasiness to words. I force myself to answer their questions, which are my burning interrogations" (BD 204). Words *as beings* thus enable Jabès to avoid in his writing the static authority which traditional textual devices (chronology, character, narrative teleology) necessarily impose. As Bounoure says, they bring questions rather than answers to the text because of their inherent ambiguity and instability; they are tyrants, according to Guglielmi, who continually defer the solution to the textual enigma.[14] Yet the tyranny they exercise, granted Jabès's literary aesthetic, is salubrious. Once personified, they enter into a textual contract as fictional collaborators, engendering interrogation much like Jabès's rabbis, gradually becoming more familiar both to the writer and to the reader: "One can trust only those words that one knows—that know us" (P 50). In view of this strange role they play, I should like to examine a few of the possible reasons for Jabès's extraordinary personification of the word.

First and foremost among these is the notion that the word is the original human artifact, that it has served humankind, and continues to do so, as a privileged tool of self-expression.[15] Hence Rosmarie Waldrop is led to postulate the specular nature of the word: as a means of self-knowledge its role for the human subject is that of a mirror.[16] Waldrop deploys this insight as the major term in her reading of the septology, arguing that the quest in *Le Livre des questions* is "man's quest to know himself, the book's quest to know its process." Indeed the subject searches for itself in the Jabesian text. Words are evoked, examined, linked to other words, woven into an arcane verbal combinatorics in the hope of locating identity: "Show me all the transformations of the sign. It could be that I find my name among them" (BY 204, RL 70).

The classical imperative of self-knowledge, however, the *gnothi seauton* and the positivist faith upon which it relies, is largely attenuated in the contemporary text. One of the most characteristic commonplaces of modernist and postmodernist literature is the denial that the subject can ever accede to an adequate representation of itself. Often the device used to convey this denial is the mirror scene; most typically, the subject, looking into the mirror, fails to recognize the reflected image. This testifies to a generalized alienation and, more important, to a schism within the subject itself, exile from the world and from oneself. This scene has imposed itself imperially upon writing in our time. Jabès formulates that commonplace far more subtly than most writers. "The word is in man's image: therefore, an other" (BD 302), he says, unequivocally stating the specular relation of man and word only to subvert it radically, arguing the distanciation of the subject from itself. In this remark, he again echoes one of his literary touchstones, Rimbaud: "*Je* est un autre."

The title of a chapter in *Elya* constitutes another variation on this theme. In "The Broken Mirror of Words" (YE 134, E 26), Jabès again adumbrates the inadequacy of words as specular devices, suggesting that the reflection they offer is splintered and fragmented, thus insufficient, and that the fault lies precisely within the words themselves. The rupture is clearly analogous to other catastrophic events in human experience from Babel to Auschwitz[17] and recapitulates them as, for Jabès, the broken mirror of words recalls the shattered Tablets of Law, the broken Vessels of the Covenant. Like the writer, condemned to labor upon an impossible Book, the human subject is condemned continually, as if lost and wandering in a carnival funhouse, to contemplate itself in distorting mirrors. Here again, words exert over human beings a tyrannical dominion whose implicit metaphor is not that of the fortress, but rather that of the prison: "You cannot free yourself of a word. The word is your birth and your death" (BQ 101, LQ 109).

As in synchrony the word serves as mirror of humanity, so in diachrony it serves as memory of the individual subject and of the species. Here is another consideration motivating Jabès to accord it personification and inhabitual status in his work. "You must not think words are without memory" (YE 203, A 105), he says. "Words come to us from the past, and to the past they return" (LB 64, EL 75). Each individual word is an archaeological artifact, a vestige of some human experience; in their impossible aggregate, in the Book, they would testify to the entire history of the species, in effect, recreating humankind.

Edmond Jabès's meditation upon the memory of words is bound up in the notion of origin, which complicates it considerably. For, as words succeed each other in pointing back toward the past, history and the words that remember it become ever more distant. At the logical end of this process is the origin of experience and the original word.

For Bounoure, original language still resounds in words; each word embodies traces of the purity and symmetry of original language, bears some distant resemblance to the sufficiency of the language of the covenant.[18] In his view, poetry is the language of origins, a fortiori the poetry of Edmond Jabès; the poet's role is to recreate the immense divine discourse of origin. Poet as mystic, as oracle: "The mystery of words, as revealed to the poet, contains the secret of everything, of this world of anxious, isolated things which gaze toward us, waiting for man to speak."[19] As categorical and optimistic as Bounoure seems to be about the possibility of recreating original language, the *how* of this problematic remains less than clear. Indeed, to the question of the roots and sources of language being irretrievably lost, he responds with another question: "Who will answer this vague, distressing question, around which clamor the words of the poems?"[20]

His strategy imitates Jabès's, but Jabès is far less sanguine about poetry's potential, far more radical in deferring origin. Jabès cloaks the origin, like the end, in successive layers of aporia. It may exist, but its existence is rendered largely irrelevant since it is unattainable; origin remains an operative construct in his work only because the poet (and humanity along with him) vainly yearns for it and strives toward it. In effect, then, the rupture of the word in Jabès is complete.

Richard Stamelman locates this rupture in the breaking of the Tablets of Law: the tablets that replaced them were written in fallen language, in words that necessarily inscribe the mutual alienation of God and man.[21] Consequently, he argues, "The text exists in a state of vacancy and *déracinement* profoundly different from the state of plenitude that once prevailed in the pre-exilic, prelapsarian homeland of the divine word. It is intimately joined to a temporal world whose precariousness and discontinuity it echoes."[22] Guglielmi concurs, although his reasoning takes a different path. Postulating the book as a tributary of the word rather than the inverse, Guglielmi suggests that, in the absence of a first book, there is no transcendental model that would allow the poet to attain "the lustral rigor of the *first word*."[23]

Both these interpretations are consistent with Jabès's own thought. Word does function as human memory, and human existence shall continue to be bound up in words. Consequently, in a very real sense, word and man are identical: "The word *is* man, his memory and his fate" (BD 302). Yet like word as mirror, the word as memory offers no hope of definitive transformation of the human condition, no firm promise of elaborating the Book. For as the poet searches through the lexicon in which memory is reflected, the image he faces is fragmented, an image that puts into *question* the linearity and coherence of human experience, annihilating that which it proposes to represent: "Memories of words. Words unhinge memory" (BD 164).

If Jabès unconditionally denies any possibility of transcendence in the process of questioning, impossibly far from both origin and end, he does not deny the process itself. On the contrary, the species confirms and guarantees its survival through the insistent questioning of words. For Jabès, argues Eric Gould, writing is "survival in the desert of words."[24] This theme is particularly insistent in *Le Livre de Yukel*, where human existence is continually tested in the crucibles of catastrophe, madness, and despair. Beyond his suicide, beyond Sarah's death, Yukel invokes his own discourse as proof of Sarah's continued existence: "I speak. Is this not proof that you exist?" (BY 21, LY 21). Words for Yukel are far more than disincarnate abstractions; they are tokens of life which vouchsafe the survival of the individual. Speech and (more important) writing are necessary, crucially so, for the life of the individual is contingent upon verbal activity, as it is upon breathing. What is true of the individual also holds for the species: "The race dies with the last word" (BY 89, LY 95). Yukel tells Sarah that, stripped of everything else, the word is their only remaining possession (BY 25, LY 26) and later assures her that this alone will suffice: "As long as we are not chased from our words we have nothing to fear. As long as our utterances keep their sound we have a voice. As long as our words keep their sense we have a soul" (BY 93, LY 99–100).

Yukel's faith in the word is his most characteristic attribute.[25] In view of the highly specular nature of Jabès's writing, Yukel's meditations on the word must be accorded exceptional privilege, for he, too, is a writer. He reflects on the ability of the word to destabilize the human subject, while itself remaining stable, affording man his only chance of existence; he suggests that the word precedes man in time, puts the universe into question *for* man, and allows man to create himself (BY 58, LY 62). Evoking a combinatory hierarchy that recurs frequently elsewhere in Jabès's work, Yukel enunciates the moral imperative of verbal activity: "A word joins other words in order to further first of all the sentence, then the page, and finally the book. In order to survive it must take an active part in freeing the world of speech, must be a dynamic agent of its transformation and unity" (BY 59, LY 63–64).

Yukel's meditation on the word and the possibilities he sees in it reflect one aspect of Jabès's poetics of the word. Yukel, too, is capable of seeing in the word a "consecrated healer" (YE 109, Y 153), a healing agent enabling the poet to repair rupture and discontinuity. This is the "fortress" side of his reflection, word as secure dwelling place. "Enter into my speech, my dark home" (BY 46, LY 50), he says, inviting the reader into the text; word as text, text as book, book as Book. Writing, for him, inaugurates a new day with each sign, a day that the word assures (DG 50, LD 80); writing is an imperative acknowledged by the poet, an imperative to save words, and thus to save himself from despair (YE 335, A 173).

Yet the darker side of Jabès's poetics of the word is omnipresent, even in the foregoing instances, situated below, beyond, or after them, nullifying the prospects they offer. As he labors to build his dwelling place, this "house of words," to borrow Guglielmi's phrase,[26] he is aware that its foundations are inadequate and that consequently the edifice will be insufficient to his needs: "'No matter how solidly you build your house,' said Reb Alkem, 'it will always rest on sand'" (BY 101, LY 108). Once again, the dwelling place fails to offer comfort and shelter; once again, the fortress is revealed to be a prison: "So many chains whose links are vocables" (II 39).

Recognizing a prison, Yukel fails to see that it is made of words: rather, he sees words as the poet's only hope of escape from his prison: "A writer escapes with words" (BY 28, LY 29). His faith in words as adequate guarantors of liberty and survival is sharply undercut by Sarah's madness. Her condition, apparently resulting form the tyranny of the world (deportation, the camps, institutionalized murder), may also be seen to result in some measure from the tyranny of the word: "The insane person is the victim of the rebellion of words" (BD 175). Her cry is the only response she can make to that tyranny; it is a wholly averbal vocalization, a human sound emitted apart from language and in stark, terrorized opposition thereto. Just as Yukel's reassurances cannot save Sarah from madness, cannot repair her broken mind, so they fail finally to guarantee his own survival. In the dialogue of word and cry resonating through *Le Livre de Yukel*, it is the cry that we hear most clearly and hauntingly.

Here again the word is subsumed by the void: Sarah's cry is the embodiment of emptiness. The scream, pure sound, cannot be adequately transcribed onto the written page; it refuses, as it were, its share of ink, and yet it is the very sound of the voiceless Book. It betokens a series of divorces: sound from sense, word from word, subject from word, subject from subject. It is the first word and the last word, it is law, it is separation, it is death. As such, it may announce the final term in Jabès's poetics of the word.

Resulting from the progressive personification of the word in Jabès, the final term assumes as well the indeterminacy into which *vocable* is plunged, occult locus of the schism of words and things. An examination of Jabès's various glosses demonstrates that *vocable* stands in apposition to other key words in Jabès's lexicon, *unknown, void, nothingness*. Even on the level of normative language, the semantic fields of these words would seem to be close. In Jabès's idiolect, however, their reciprocal affinities are undeniable, and they function as practically interchangeable synonyms. Moreover, they immediately evoke or, as Sydney Lévy would put it, "call" to another word, *God*. The fate of the *vocable* as it assumes its status within the Book is thus linked by Jabès to some notion of God; in at least one case, he renders this explicit: "Our words [*vocables*] testify above all to divine obliteration" (YE 214, A 20). Perhaps, then, rather than saying that the problematic of the *vocable* results in aporia, in void and erasure, it would be more appropriate to say that it is deferred. Jabès's reflection upon *vocable*, and any illumination of this poetics of the word consequent upon it, is transposed within the Book from *vocable* to *God*. Granted this, an examination of the latter word is necessary.

The itinerary of the word is recapitulated in the itinerary of the subject; both follow paths of exile and wandering: "My exile has led me, syllable by syllable, to God, the most exiled of words [*vocables*]. And in Him I had a glimpse of the unity of Babel" (BY 86, LY 92). Here again, the process of transference of meaning from *vocable* to *Dieu* seems clear. On one hand, it appears to be inevitable and even harmonious: the Word, after all, is a traditional figure of the godhead, and each individual word may display some trace, some vestige of this association.[27] But two other considerations intervene to subvert any progression toward sufficiency. First, any enunciation of the divine in Jabès's work is inevitably bound up in (and considerably attenuated by) his atheism: Jabès uses the word *God* as pure dislocated metaphor.[28] Second, his allusion to Babel functions in a curious manner. For Babel marks in common mythology (and, a fortiori, in the personal mythology of a writer) a catastrophic event, a second Fall as it were, entailing the radical disunification of language. For Jabès to postulate unity in disunity is perhaps less startling than that assertion might seem under the pen of another writer, granted once again his proclivity for paradox. But the force of this passage transcends the mere subversion of truism since, like *vocable* before it, the word *God* comes to serve as the guarantor of all the other words in the lexicon.

Unity and disunity, adequacy and inadequacy: in each utterance of the word *Dieu*, a tormented oscillation between these two poles is apparent, causing the rest of the words in Jabès's writing, and indeed the

Book itself, to tremble. The word among words which should, finally, arrest and locate meaning in fact absconds from that imperative: "'The word *God* interests me,' he said, 'because it's a word that defies understanding; that, granted that it cannot be apprehended as a word, escapes from meaning, transcends the latter in order to annul it; so that there is always a word before or after the word, a word without a word, in the past or in the future; a useless word, then, whose use shocks the mind'" (LR 67). As words are piled upon the word, no resolution is reached, but rather an impression of continual resistance: defiance, escape, annulment. It is precisely this process of accretion that Jabès puts into question, testifying as it does to the infinite circularity of language. Alluding once again to the dictionary—that book wherein the tautological character of language is best exemplified—he argues: "Of all the words in the dictionary, the word *God* is the most refractory. We are never sure of the use we make of it" (P 50). Just as in the case of *vocable* the meaning of *God* is continually deferred as Jabès launches that word into wandering. Defining it on one occasion as a metaphor for the void (DL 87), he subsequently remarks that that may be the most characteristic attribute of the word: "Would *God* be the emptiest word in our vocabulary?" (P 79).

If part of Jabès's project lies, as Gould has suggested, in an effort to reinvent the divine Word, that project clearly contains the seeds of its own destruction.[29] More important still, it consciously disseminates and cultivates them. "The words that are our axis, our roots, come from a region designated by the unpronounceable Name. But these seeds produce sprouts, flowers, and fruits only if they are entrusted to a charnel earth," argues Bounoure.[30] Jabès's words long for that carnal earth as the Jew longs for the Promised Land, as the writer longs for the Book. Springing from the first abstraction, the Tetragrammaton, they largely retain its characteristics, indeterminacy and voicelessness: "The first word of the lexicon is a name, and that name contains all names, and all these names come together in that name to form none other than the only name which is a word among other equally derisory words: God" (LR 79). End figures beginning, beginning figures end; any possibility of dialectical progression is thus rigorously denied as the sign continues to wander. Bearing in mind the imperative enunciated earlier, "to abolish the graven image," the entire process of verbal representation is called radically into question. The referentiality of the *me* in the language of the covenant should serve as language's guarantor; yet, Jabès contends, it does not fill this role and is, itself, pitifully unstable. Thus, insofar as *God* continues to resound in the lexicon, all words, like Sarah's scream, shuttle along a catastrophic itinerary of exile, an infinite and irrecuperably decentered spiral, enunciating in this process a silent but nonetheless insistent discourse of pain.

Finally, then, meditation upon the lexicon shapes the thematics of the Jabesian text. Guglielmi writes, "The desert of the vocable, its character both instable and vain (negating) is one of the primordial marks of the Jabesian system."[31] Instability and vanity are the laws of the word, laws imposed upon the poet, which he in turn, through writing, formalizes in the text: "The law is in the word [*vocable*]. / I write: I apply the law" (BY 54, LY 58). In the process of "calling" from word to word, in the continual transfer and remotivation of meaning, law is inevitably and imperially subsumed by death; this is the ultimate consequence of the word: "In death, the word [*vocable*] becomes visible. It is the Law read" (BY 172, RL 36).

Word is law, law is death: as connotation leaps vertiginously from one *vocable* to another, that process is inscribed and legitimized in the formal aspect of the word. In other words, the *resemblance* of word and death on the semantic level is supported by the literal analogy of *mot* and *mort*, the confluence of the letters that compose them. Jabès, of course, is keenly aware of this resemblance and plays on it: "How many admired deaths . . . in the word [*mot*] DEATH [*mort*]" (SD 86). Here, both aspects of his poetics of the word become apparent. Death is exponentially inscribed in the word, but that very iteration tends to negate it: the word thus simultaneously entails the accretion of death upon death and also the death *of* death, or survival: "Perhaps writing means revealing the word to yourself at death's threshold" (YE 337, A 175).

The poet thus plays precariously in the "*derisory* abyss of words,"[32] in the locus of their infinite regression, constraining tenuous meaning through the tension of difference and resemblance: "There is a meaning of the word which leads to another meaning, which in turn leads to a third, which allows us to see that we are still only at the threshold of the word" (DD 18). No perspective of ingress is offered to the poet at the end of his itinerary, for it is endless. However exhausting and meticulous is his interrogation of the verbal artifact, he is condemned to hover continually at the threshold of the word, just as the book he labors to elaborate is condemned to hover at the threshold of the Book: "We write while words keep moving away" (YE 265, A 80).

the story

*Writing means going on a
journey, at the end of which you will
not be the same,
    at the bottom of the page filled.*
(BQ 169, LQ 186)

As questions engender questions, the interrogative mode of Edmond Jabès's writing has given rise to a variety of inquiries. Faced with the hermeticism, the indeterminacy, and the intense specularity of *Le Livre des questions* and *Le Livre des ressemblances*, many critics have chosen (wisely, I think) to perpetuate that interrogative mode in their own reading strategies, spinning webs of query around given problematics.[1] Salient among these problematics is the question of absence, which resonates throughout Jabès's work, playing among the iso-topies, vigorously resisting definitive response. Curiously enough, several critics have argued that the principal absence in Jabès's writing is the one thing that would *seem* to be most demonstrably present. Paul Auster, suggesting the analogy of the Jabesian text and a *deus absconditus*, says, "Like the hidden God of classic Jewish theology, the text exists only by virtue of its absence"; Rosmarie Waldrop states categorically, "The text is missing"; and, changing terms, Sydney Lévy declares, "Strangely, what is missing from Edmond Jabès's books is precisely the book."[2]

Taken at face value, the notion seems absurd: a glassy-eyed literalist would undoubtedly ask Waldrop, for instance, how she managed to produce her excellent translations of Jabès if the text is missing. The notion is nonetheless provocative and constitutes, perhaps, a polemical response to the accretion of absences in Jabès; it is all the more provocative, moreover, insofar as there seems to be a fair degree of consensus concerning it. There may be another means of dealing with the problem of absence in this body of work: one might launch another interrogative series, beginning with the question of presence. What does one look to find in Jabès? Where are the reader's expectations of presence most radically frustrated? What aspect of the text, having absconded, would lead a critic to call into question the presence of the text itself?

Judging from recent readings of Jabès, the problem of narrative mode may furnish the most reasonable point of departure in an examination of these questions. Since, as readers struggle to engage the Jabesian text, the problem of narrative mode seems to be the most common obstacle, I should like to propose an inquiry into that problem as it manifests itself in the first volume of *Le Livre des questions*, entitled (in apparent redundancy) *Le Livre des questions*.[3] More precisely still, I should like to concentrate on a story that may or may not be told in that text, the story of Sarah and Yukel.[4]

Two brief summaries of this story offer some idea of its importance, as well as the interpretive problems it engenders. The first is from Paul Auster:

At the core of The Book of Questions *there is a story—a separation of two young lovers, Sarah and Yukel, during the time of the Nazi deportations. Yukel is a writer—described as the "witness" who serves as Jabès's alter ego and whose words are often indistinguishable from his; Sarah is a young woman who is shipped to a concentration camp and who returns insane. But the story is never really told, and it in no way resembles a traditional narrative.*[5]

The second is from Jabès himself:

At the center of each of these books [the first three volumes of Le Livre des questions*] there is a story, the story of two adolescents . . . two lovers who are deported. They return from the camps; she has gone mad, and her cries become indistinguishable from the cries of a persecuted people, a people persecuted over the centuries; in the second volume he commits suicide, and everything takes place as if after his death.*[6]

Several things are to be remarked here. First, Auster and Jabès use metaphors to situate the locus of the story in the text: *core, center.* Auster seems to suggest that the story of Sarah and Yukel lies *within* the text, largely obscured by it, isospherically central and thus seminal. His notion is similar to Raymond Queneau's text-as-onion, the progressive layers being peeled away in the process of exegesis.[7] Jabès's metaphor is more troubling still in light of his insistent propensity to decentralize.[8] Jabès takes extraordinary pains, throughout his work, to deny the existence of the center as an operative construct, to subvert related or ancillary notions such as essence and generative locus. Why, then, this contradiction, this primacy accorded to the story of Sarah and Yukel?

Two problems become apparent in the juxtaposition of these summaries: the problem of variant versions and the question of prominencing. Both accounts attempt to distill the story as far as possible, to recount it in a few lines; both Auster and Jabès elaborate their accounts in function of this reductive constraint. Yet their summaries are different, and some of the differences are quite striking. Jabès, for instance, tells us that Sarah and Yukel are deported; Auster mentions only Sarah's deportation. Assuming (for the moment at least) Jabès's *authority*, does Auster's summary constitute a variant version, or has he merely chosen to accord prominence to one element of the story rather than to another? Whichever it might be, what aspect (or aspects) of *Le Livre des questions* might account for this difference? Both Auster and Jabès violate the strictly intradiegetic frame, but in different ways. Jabès insists on Sarah's "screams," suggesting their transcendent relation to the Holocaust and to the history of the persecution of the Jews. Auster mentions that Yukel is a writer, pointing toward his relation to Jabès and the problem of the indeterminacy of narrative voice in the text. He argues that the story of Sarah and Yukel "is never really told." These *écarts* are all the more significant in view of the reductive constraint inherent in the process of summarization. Into a form that demands a minimum of digression from the object summarized both Jabès and Auster have injected explicit commentary. This is perhaps an inevitable aspect of summary, indeed of version (whether the commentary be explicit or implicit); nonetheless, the degree of variance is astonishing and undoubtedly directly consequent upon narrative problems in *Le Livre des questions*: Auster's argument that the story of Sarah and Yukel "in no way resembles a traditional narrative" is elegantly understated. Granted all of this, it may become clear why I chose to furnish Auster's and Jabès's summaries rather than hazard my own. The choice of Sarah and Yukel's story may seem somewhat less arbitrary in view of the importance accorded to it by Jabès himself and by one of his most lucid readers.

In *Le Livre des questions*, the notion of a story is itself put into question, through persistent and highly specular commentary:

> *"What is the story of the book?"*
> *"Becoming aware of a scream."* (BQ 16, LQ 14)

The question is posed, an answer is tendered; but the answer is less than satisfactory, insofar as it perpetuates the question, contributing to what Roland Barthes called the hermeneutic code of the text.[9] The words *tale* and *story*, insistently recurring in the text, are refused any referential determinacy as they oscillate between the poles defined by *book* and *question*:

"Do we have a tale here?"
"My story has been told so many times."
"What is your story?"
"Ours, insofar as it is absent [elle est absente]."
"I do not understand."
"Speaking tortures me." (BQ 18, LQ 16)

Within the text, the origin of the questions is indeterminate; clearly, however, they resemble the questions a reader might ask in his or her efforts to decipher the hermeneutic code. Moreover, each "response" involves a swerve away from direct response, introducing new elements, themselves indeterminate (what, for instance, are the referents of *my* and *ours*?), thus engendering new questions. The context of the discourse is obscure; even when words seem to be referential, who or what they refer to may be undeterminable; the referent of *elle* seems to be *story*, but *elle* might just as well refer to Sarah. The problematic of presence and absence is inscribed within the passage and explicitly associated with the problem of the story. The tension of that opposition engenders and then reflects that of the mode of narration itself, and the consequent communicational insufficiency is figured in the verb *tortures*.

One questioning voice in the text (or, possibly, many) constantly demands information, which is furnished only obliquely, offered and withheld at the same time. Even when it seems that coherent information is about to be offered, it is immediately subverted as the responding voice swerves back into the domain of indeterminacy: "The story of Sarah and Yukel is the account, through various dialogues and meditations attributed to imaginary rabbis, of a love destroyed by men and words. It has the dimensions of the book and the bitter stubbornness of a wandering question" (BQ 26, LQ 26). The narrative imperative is, as it were, recognized, but it is resolutely (and progressively) refused. The sign continues to slip: *account*, like *story*, is reinserted into its strange oscillation between presence and absence, between *book* and *question*. The story of Sarah and Yukel is obviously conditioned by this phenomenon, by the apparent refusal of the narrative act. Thus the demands placed on the reader of *Le Livre des questions* are contradictory: on one hand, the principal element of the hermeneutic code functions to coax the reader toward a painstaking reconstruction of the story of Sarah and Yukel; on the other, much of the metanarrative commentary explicitly denies the possibility of such an enterprise. Even as the story is announced, the text warns the reader away from it: "In these pages, little will be said about Yukel Serafi" (BQ 53, LQ 54). And the questioning voice persists in demanding more information, protesting a lack, an absence: "You hardly talked about Sarah and Yukel" (BQ 122, LQ 132).

The story of Sarah and Yukel is "told" in fragments, in elliptical snatches.[10] Isolated references to their first meeting recur in the text: "Yukel, that evening I could not stand my room any more than you yours. Did I know beforehand that I would run into you at the corner of my street? I walked straight ahead. You came to meet me" (BQ 114, LQ 123); "She does not know any more if he followed her. They had slowed down as if, together, they had become aware of a possible future" (BQ 157, LQ 173). In its telling, their story refuses chronology; an allusion to Yukel's deportation, "I see you again in my hotel room, so upset by my departure" (BQ 136, LQ 150), precedes an allusion to an anterior event:

One morning when we were lying on the beach, she traced her
initials in the sand with her forefinger.

S.S.

Sarah Schwall.

S.S.

S.S.

(BQ 145, LQ 159)

The conflict of the narrating and the narrated is part of the more general subversion of traditionalist narrative norms in *Le Livre des questions*, of course, and, like the indeterminacy of narrative voice, functions within the hermeneutic code. The elliptical nature of the telling is clear, moreover, in the preceding passage: Sarah and Yukel's descent into the Holocaust is implicit in Sarah's anthroponymic tattoo. An analogous technique is used a bit further on, as the general becomes fiercely juxtaposed to the particular:

When the yellow star was shining in the sky of the accursed, he wore the sky on his chest. The sky of youth with its wasp's sting, and the sky with the armband of mourning.

He was seventeen. An age with wide margins. (BQ 155, LQ 171)

References to their life in the camps are equally sparse and elliptical: "I am thinking of you with my new chains. I see you with eyes that have plunged into hell" (BQ 147, LQ 161); "From her deported parents as well as from her companions in captivity, Sarah inherited the stubbornness of her race" (BQ 147, LQ 176). Narrative chronology is further blurred as Yukel conflates past and present in his memory after his return from the camps: "He thinks of his sister dead in his arms, of the locked asphyxiated land, of all the dead who delight in Sarah's madness, of Sarah, dead in the life of grain and fruit" (BQ 170, LQ 187). The problem of extracting details about Sarah and Yukel, shorn as they are of coherent, supportive context, is considerably complicated by the general indeterminacy of narrative voice in *Le Livre des questions*. It gradually becomes apparent that two of the voices composing the narrative fabric are those of Sarah and Yukel themselves. But each speaks in many different tones, corresponding to the different stages of the story. Yukel's status in the text is particularly ambiguous; Auster identifies him as Jabès's alter ego, but his role is, I think, far more complex than that. Both Sarah and Yukel are presented as storytellers: "Tell me about Yukel Serafi, father. I love his stories" (BQ 158, LQ 175). In a rare (and consequently startling) intervention of traditional narrative in the text, the reader is furnished with information about Sarah's past: "When she was fourteen, Sarah wanted to be a teacher. Instead of joining her classmates on holidays, she gathered children around her, whom she taught to use words (to let themselves be caught by them), whom she told stories of light and dark. They listened, as one might listen to the colors of the world monologuing until evening" (BQ 155–56, LQ 172). The relation of this passage to the text as a whole is specular, and the image is diametrically inverted: this is how Sarah told stories before her deportation and consequent madness; this is how stories (including that in *Le Livre des questions*) might have been told, had not the Holocaust intervened.

The fact that both Sarah and Yukel are storytellers, narrators, makes it still more difficult to determine the diegetic limits of their story. At various moments in the text, as should be clear from the passages cited, both function (to borrow Gérard Genette's terms) as intradiegetic-homodiegetic narrators, narrators in the second degree who tell their own story.[11] But the chronological point of emanation of their discourse is not localized with respect to the story: the narrative chronotopos, like the other components of narrative mode in *Le Livre des questions*, is constantly shifting. Moreover, Yukel also functions as an extradiegetic-homodiegetic narrator, a narrator in the first degree:

"You are the narrator, Yukel. From book to book, from sky to sky."

"I am the stranger."

"Yukel, tell us the story of the stranger."

"I speak,

and you see through me,

you learn through my words,

and you follow the traitor who passes himself off as the servant, and without whom, alas (just as the giddy wind for the stem whose flower it tore off), Yukel, the stranger, would be nothing on earth but the nameless and unnecessary display of an instant of the unutterable distress." (BQ 123, LQ 133)

On still another level, Yukel is explicitly presented as a writer; one result of his writing may be much of *Le Livre des questions* itself (or some avatar thereof in the infinite regression of book within book). Statements such as "My books are made to be read first, then told. That is why I call them tales" (BQ 63, LQ 66) may be attributed to Yukel, to Jabès, or to any one of a regressive series of implied intermediate authors. The ambiguity of Yukel's narrative status thus contributes most forcefully to the ambiguity of narrative mode in the text.

Still, the principal question remains, Why is the story of Sarah and Yukel told in this fashion? First and perhaps most obvious, Jabès, as a contemporary avant-garde writer, has the weight of recent literary history to contend with. After the experimentation of the *nouveau roman* and the innovations it engendered, an avant-gardist can hardly return to a traditionalist mode of narration; when Barthes praised the "writerly" quality of Alain Robbe-Grillet's work, he argued the bankruptcy of the "readerly" text.[12] This and other polemics in the late 1950s and early 1960s must surely have influenced Jabès, however minimally. He has alluded to the representational fallacy and the problem of prominencing as key considerations in the writing of *Le Livre des questions*: "To tell a story, in my opinion, is to lose it. If I tell you about my life in detail, for example, it escapes in the details I have chosen to recount. In life you have no choice. How do you know what is most important? A story limits the life of a person to the things someone else has to say about him."[13] The problem becomes, thus, a *question* of telling-without-telling, which is, in a nutshell, the narrative paradox of *Le Livre des questions*. Contradictory forces are at work in the text, a narrative impulse conflicts with an impulse toward antinarrative; this conflict would seem to have been vigorously operative in the genesis of the text:

Little by little, as if in spite of me, this thing began to emerge, the book I had been pursuing in total darkness began to take shape . . . by means of questioning, by means of a dramatic story I wanted to present in the same way I felt it inside me, a story I wanted to tell without ever really telling it. It was as if there were stories that didn't have to be told in order to be known and understood. And this was quite new in a formal sense: that wasn't the way you were supposed to tell a story. But the idea of a story in itself didn't satisfy me . . . that really wasn't what I was after. But around the story I had in mind, there was the questioning, and more and more that became what haunted me about the book.[14]

Questioning, the questions posed by Yukel, by Sarah, by the imaginary rabbis, is one way to avoid assuming the authority that traditionalist narrative necessarily entails. And, as author, one of Jabès's most insistent theoretical intents is radically to question the notion of authority within the book.[15] This tactic, too, is generative of paradox; if Jabès can state (as we have seen) that the story of Sarah and Yukel is at the "center" of *Le Livre des questions*, he can also state that "it is the questioning around the story that gives the story its dimension. But the story is there only as a kind of basic pretext."[16] The latter expression is richly evocative: again, in describing the function of this story within the book, Jabès seems to contradict himself, insofar as elsewhere he insists on the nonexistence of the fundamental, the essential, the basic. The word *pretext*, derived from the Latin *praetexere*, to weave in front, to pretend, to disguise, suggests that the story of Sarah and Yukel is offered as a superficial motive concealing a real one. In both French and English, the word, through homophony, may draw the reader toward another consideration, a pre-text, or some object antecedent to the text. This function of the word, as contradictory as it may sound given Jabès's ulterior discourse, is reinforced by Jabès's own account of the genesis of *Le Livre des questions*. The notion of the preexistence of the story, the notion that it once existed integrally, only to be deconstructed in the process of writing *Le Livre des questions*, is implicit in Jabès's authorial strategy: it is also implicit in the efforts of some of his readers, urged on by the strong hermeneutic code, to reconstruct that story.

The notion is less outlandish than it might seem since the story of Sarah and Yukel is also a story of the Holocaust. As Jabès says, "For the Jews, unfortunately, after all the camps and all the horrors, it is an all too banal story. It isn't necessary to go into details. When you say: they were deported—that is enough for a Jew to understand the *whole* story."[17] This may help to explain why the story of Sarah and Yukel is represented in such a fragmentary, sparse, elliptical manner. But broader aesthetic and political considerations necessarily impose themselves. Their story *is* banal, in that it resembles thousands of other stories. And why, after all, should one elaborate a fictional account when so many historical accounts exist, when so many actual lives and deaths are still waiting to be chronicled? What is the relation between the general and the particular, or, to put it another way, what can link the collective experience of the Holocaust and the experience of individual people, be the latter fictive or real? To what degree can an individual story exemplify a historical reality as overwhelming as the Holocaust? Is fiction a proper vehicle for this exemplification? Berel Lang has addressed this problem as it arises in Jabès's work:

We understand here the dilemma that Jabès—and any writer who takes the Holocaust as subject—confronts. On the one hand, it is difficult, perhaps impossible, for a writer to meet the Holocaust face to face, to represent it. The events themselves are too large for the selective mirror of fiction, too transparent for the unavoidable conceits of literary figuration; linguistic representation is in any case redundant, thus an impediment, when the events that converge on a subject speak directly and clearly for themselves. On the other hand, to write about the Holocaust obliquely, by assumption, leaves the task that had been declined by the author to the reader, who can hardly—if the writer will not—hope to find a passage from personal emotion and imagery to artifice. Where then is the work of literary representation to be done?[18]

Perhaps it will not be done in poetry: in the mid-1950s, Theodor Adorno stated that "to write poetry after Auschwitz is barbaric."[19] Although he reconsidered that position a decade later, his initial statement had an enormous effect, particularly among Jewish writers, and continues to do so.[20] The principal resonance of his statement is moral and proscriptive: any aesthetic representation of the Holocaust being necessarily a trivialization of the latter, one *must not* attempt such a representation. But there is another moral imperative at work in this problematic, in direct opposition to Adorno's. Raymond Federman, a Jewish writer and a survivor of the camps, has enunciated it in the following terms: "The writer, however, the Jewish writer at any rate, cannot, must not evade his moral responsibilities, we are told, nor can he avoid dealing with his Jewishness. It is demanded of him. And the writer himself feels obligated to tell and retell the sad story, lest we forget. He must become the historian of the Holocaust. He must tell the truth—the 'real story.' But how? That is the fundamental question that confronts us today."[21]

In its dissemination, Adorno's position has given rise to polemics concerning not only the moral impossibility of writing on the Holocaust but the *literal* impossibility as well. The argument is that the Holocaust, like the Fall, like Babel, is an event that marks human experience in such a fashion that language becomes, forever after, inadequate; that is, language is no longer sufficient to our expressive needs. Both Federman and Lang deploy this double problem in considering Jabès; Federman sees him as "perhaps the only Jewish writer who implicitly acknowledges in his work the impossibility of speech when dealing with the Holocaust and the concentration camps."[22] Lang argues that Jabès avoids the double question: "It is thus, unhappily, repressed—this question of whether writing centered in the Holocaust, the Nazi genocide of the Jews, is even possible: literally and morally *possible*."[23] Although both are highly suggestive, neither of these views is a fair characterization of Jabès's position on this problem. *Le Livre des questions*, like Jabès's other work, puts the linguistic sign into question but simultaneously testifies to the author's faith in that sign.[24] Regarding the possibility of writing on the Holocaust, Jabès, in a response to Adorno's dictum, has rendered his position unequivocally clear: "To

Adorno, the German philosopher, who has said that we cannot write after Auschwitz, I say that we must write. But we cannot write like before."[25]

Question, commentary, fragment are some of the formal components of this difference. Auster, arguing that the story of Sarah and Yukel cannot be told, suggests that the commentaries in *Le Livre des questions* constitute investigations "of a text that has not been written";[26] Waldrop operates this same sort of displacement when she states, "Commentary is the main procedure of *The Book of Questions*, commentary on a story that is not told except through the commentary."[27] But the commentary, more precisely the nature of the commentary, in *Le Livre des questions* is directly related to the thematics of the story of Sarah and Yukel. Susan Handelman has pointed out the similarities of Jabès's technique and that of canonical texts in the Jewish tradition.[28] Jabès's imaginary rabbis engage in much the same activity as the thinkers who contributed to the Mishnah and the Gemara, although the former direct their questions and commentaries toward the story of Sarah and Yukel, rather than the Torah. As paradoxical as it may seem, Jabès has appealed, in his search for a different sort of writing that would permit him to tell his tale, to a familiar and highly codified body of work. In addition to this formal analogy, Handelman notes another point of convergence between the Jabesian text and Talmud, insofar as both assume the prior existence of the story: "The story is already known without having to retell it, and yet problematic enough that it has to be constantly restudied and rethought—and also so revered that it must always be retold."[29] Noting, further, the influence of Hasidism on Jabès, Handelman likens him to a Hasidic rebbe: a storyteller, a dealer in parable, whose tales, although already known, are constantly retold for the edification of the community. The analogy is striking, for within the Hasidic tradition (which relies heavily on the tale), there seems to be no interdiction against telling-the-Holocaust. Indeed, Yaffa Eliach has collected such tales; one of her sources, Rabbi Israel Spira, at the close of a particularly harrowing account of the Janowska

Road Camp, alludes to the same moral imperative Federman mentioned: "'God manages a strange world; at times it is difficult to comprehend,' the rabbi reflected as if to himself as he told the story some thirty years later in his Brooklyn home. 'Yet it is our duty to tell the story over and over again. Telling the tales is an attempt to understand and come to terms with a most difficult reality.'"[30] In this perspective, telling the story, continuing to tell, is an affirmation of survival. If one accepts the argument (advanced by Derrida and, later, by Robert Duncan) that the Jews are, in some sense, the People of the Story, telling-the-Holocaust testifies to the survival not only of individuals but of a collectivity and its tradition.[31]

Jabès has said that *his* tale, *Le Livre des questions*, must be read as a *récit éclaté*, a fragmented story.[32] This formal innovation would seem to have one very obvious function in that the fragment serves as an objective correlative: the historical dystopia of the Holocaust is reflected in the narrative dystopia of the Jabesian text.[33] For narrative typically abhors questions, commentary, and fragmentation. Clearly, Jabès is dealing in an antinarrative, a painstaking subversion of traditional narrative norms. But those norms impose themselves on the writing process; granted the burden of literary tradition and the nature of the story, there is a strong impulse toward coherent telling at work in *Le Livre des questions* as the text oscillates between two poles: "Does writing a book not mean to make and unmake it at the same time?"[34] This oscillation is best exemplified in the story of Sarah and Yukel: story as "center" of text, story as "pretext." Its rhythm is incremental: as the text progresses, the narrative imperative becomes stronger. The questions become more insistent, and the responding voice's reluctance to tell is gradually eroded:

Yes, but there must be more? "He had a daughter, Sarah . . ." Yes, but there must be more? "He was called 'the Jew,' and his wife and daughter, 'the wife and daughter of the Jew.'" Yes, yes, but there must be more? "He had lost his faith . . . He no longer knew who he was . . . He was French . . . decorated . . .

His wife and daughter were French . . ." Yes, but there must be more?
"Sometimes, he spoke in public to brand racism, to affirm the rights of
man . . ." Yes, yes, but there must be more? "He died in a gas chamber
outside France . . . and his wife died in a gas chamber outside France . . . and
his daughter came back to France, out of her mind." (BQ 167, LQ 184)

There is no explosion of truth here, but rather the result of a catastrophic process of interrogation, that point at which the resisting
voice, in spite of its determination, must cede to constraint, announc-
ing as it does so the final questions of this book:

Have you seen how a kingdom is made and unmade?
Have you seen how a book is made and unmade? (BQ 175, LQ 193)

Q....

t h e   b o o k

The work I write
immediately rewrites itself
in the book.

(YE 323, A 157)

In dynamic, combinatory play, the disparate elements of Edmond Jabès's poetics converge upon his construct of constructs, the book. Just as the interrogation of the letter defines the ground upon which Jabès erects his meditation on the word; as the word functions in turn as the foundation of the story told and untold; so Jabès builds his most imposing dwelling, the book, upon highly codified sets of tributary figures. "To speak about Jabès today, one must necessarily address the problematic of the book, in all its complexity," states Joseph Guglielmi.[1] He is right on two fronts. First and most obvious, Jabès's discourse on the book is as nearly inevitable in character as it is possible for any given literary topos to be: it is by far the most insistent theme in his work. Paradoxically, this discourse serves both to identify Jabès's writing with the postmodernist specular text and, through its very amplification, to distinguish Jabès from his contemporaries, to guarantee his originality. It imposes itself so imperially upon the reader that it is difficult to imagine a critical act of reasonably broad scope wherein no attempt is made to come to terms with it; quite simply (as Guglielmi suggests), it is necessary to account for Jabès's vision of the book. Second, Guglielmi is correct in pointing out the "extreme complexity" of this notion. In his literary strategy, Edmond Jabès wagers heavily on various techniques of overdetermination: the signifiers that undergo such a process (words, figures, images) assume new roles in the grid of resemblance erected by the Jabesian text. This is, of course, a highly idiosyncratic process of becoming, which reaches its culmination in the construct of the book, the most overdetermined element in the textual fabric.

For the critic, the very complexity of the construct poses problems that may not be readily apparent. That complexity results from a painstaking process of semiotic remotivation on Jabès's part; it accounts in large measure for the construct's aesthetic efficacy. Any interpretive act must necessarily minimize this complexity: the hermeneute unravels knots, analyzes, dismembers. Short of rewriting an author's text, like Pierre Menard, one cannot hope to escape this, but it is incumbent upon the critic to take pains to assure that reduction does not give way to trivialization. Accordingly, in my examination of the problematic of the book, I shall propose one initial reduction of the construct for the purposes of analysis, drawing a distinction between the Book in the ideal, the abstract, and the book as it is manifested concretely in Jabès's writings; some significance will be found, I think, in the points of articulation between the two.

Jabès himself invokes this distinction with considerable insistence, repeatedly interrogating the reciprocal relations of Book and book: "Would the Book of books derive from the potential of all other books?" (LR 89). The former looms above and beyond the latter, object of longing and of obsessional nostalgia, impossible model. The Book asserts itself imperiously, but it is never manifest. It is lost: "All books would be merely flawed images of the lost book" (LR 49); it is hidden: "The book depends upon the hope of a resemblance to 'the hidden Book'" (LR 87); it is suspended, in latent form, within the book: "These pages of reflections, of obstinate interrogations—reflecting and questioning being nothing other, perhaps, than furnishing a form to thought—are merely the retained leaves of a book, suspended within the book itself" (P 14). In each case, the Book is impossibly distant: in time (it is an ancient artifact), in space (its locus is undiscoverable), and, most characteristically, in its pale imitation.

The last image is highly pertinent. Jabès alludes repeatedly to "the Book within the book," suggesting that the Book hovers in its material analogue, present yet unattainable. The material book is thus a structure of infinite regression, a *mise-en-abyme* wherein each step taken toward the ideal entails a further obscuring of that ideal. Even in full cognizance of the impossibility of any eventual union, each writing act, suggests Jabès, strains toward the Book: "This is a book or, rather, the hope for a book written and rewritten night after night, as if it could not come about by writing alone, as if it were happening elsewhere, far from my pen, without my patiently awaited words, with other words, other dreams, by other routes, during other rests, with other screams, but with the same silence" (YE 14, Y 21). It is precisely in this dynamic, this straining, that the presence of the Book may be inferred: it is after all a question of traces, the traces of a pure, prelapsarian ideal in a fallen world. Those traces are the loci of articulation between Book and book, where the real business of writing, argues Jabès, takes place: "There would then be two books in one. The book within the book— austere, elusive, sacred Book—and the book which offers itself to our curiosity, a profane work, but one whose transparence, here and there, reveals the presence of the Book hidden within" (PL 54).

Adolfo Fernandez Zoïla feels that this articulation is the crux of Jabès's poetics and suggests that it is dialogic in character.[2] His insight is provocative, especially in light of the privileged status dialogue enjoys in Jabès's work: dialogue subverts the authority of narrative, it decenters voice, it furnishes a space for equivocality and interrogation. Much like the fragment, it allows for an *approach* to the Book without pretending to the totality or unity that, according to Jabès, are realized only in the Book itself and never in its material imitations.

The sources of Jabès's vision of the book are multiple and varied. To return to a distinction that he himself frequently draws, one might say that there are both sacred and profane antecedents, respectively lodged in the Judaic tradition and in a certain literary tradition to which Jabès willingly refers. François Laruelle has characterized this phenomenon with the figure of chiasmus: "Jabès's work is located at the intersection of the Greco-Occidental consecration of the Book as the level of literary immanence, and of the Jewish interpretation of the Book's transcendence, of its nothingness, of its illegibility. At the intersection—at the chiasmus perhaps—of the *solicitude* for the Book as the Being of the being-of-the-book, and of the Jewish *passion* for the book and its loftiness."[3] Once again, a dialogic structure seems to be at work. Just as the Book and the book continually "call" to each other, as Sydney Lévy would put it,[4] so the Aristotelian tradition and the Judaic tradition are alternately voiced in Edmond Jabès's call for the Book.

This dialogic structure is recapitulated within both the sacred and the profane, since two principal bodies of speculation are apparent within each. In the domain of the sacred, these are Talmud and cabala; the profane voices are those of Stéphane Mallarmé and Maurice Blanchot. In his conversations with Marcel Cohen, Jabès refers to the Talmud as the book of exile, based as it is on the process of questioning (DL 105); later he states explicitly that the Talmud is linked to his own pelagic conception of the Book: "The Talmudists frequently compare the

Talmud to an ocean. The very dimensions of the work resembled my own conception of the book" (DL 107). Other resemblances may be adduced: the Talmud, for instance, is a layering of gloss upon gloss,[5] a work that comes into being in the *margins*, the critical locus of writing for Jabès. It is, moreover, highly dialogic—polylogic, in fact—since it is constituted by a multiplicity of rabbinical voices; these voices find their analogues in Jabès's imaginary rabbis.

Parallel to this current of influence and, not infrequently, in agonistic opposition to it, is the cabala. Again, Jabès has deliberately inscribed this source within his construct of the Book: "Before Mallarmé—and, naturally, in a different context—the cabalists had already dreamed of an absolute book which would exclude chance, the book of perfect legibility" (DL 119). Susan Handelman has investigated the relations of Talmud and cabala (or "normative" and "mystical" Jewish tradition) in Jabès's work and has found the two to be constructively opposed therein.[6] Cabala is deeply rooted in tradition, she argues, and yet it continually tends to subvert that tradition, putting more conventional rabbinic thought into question. This struggle between convention and innovation, between scholarly erudition and mystical illumination, is highly characteristic of the Book as Edmond Jabès conceives of it.

As to the secular domain, Mallarmé's influence is clearly enormous. In our time, it would be difficult to speak of an idealist vision of the Book without alluding to Mallarmé, and Jabès freely acknowledges his influence: "Undeniably, I was influenced most heavily by Rimbaud and Mallarmé. Rimbaud, because he helped me, among other things, to read the surrealists. Mallarmé assumed his final importance for me when I discovered his obsession with the total book" (DL 27).[7] Still, Jabès takes pains to declare his independence from Mallarmé. He suggests that Mallarmé's Book was necessarily closed, in that it synthesized all books, all readings, into one, allowing neither prolongation nor interpretation. Jabès argues that this is precisely where his ideal differs from that of Mallarmé: "The notion that haunts me personally is, I think, more modest. I have always dreamed of a book which would reproduce the process of life. First it prolongs us, then it replaces us. Can you imagine that a child might one day possess the answers to all the questions that his father has asked himself? I felt then that my books should make and unmake themselves indefinitely, on behalf of the following book. Of course there is a limit, but it is that of my possibilities as a writer. It is not contained, I think, in my books" (DL 120).

More subtle but equally important is the influence of Maurice Blanchot.[8] In a broad sense, Jabès acknowledges Blanchot generously. He was grateful for and illuminated by Blanchot's early essay on his work,[9] has in turn devoted several short texts to Blanchot,[10] has used passages from the latter's work as epigraphs in his own books,[11] and indeed borrowed the title of one of these, *Ça suit son cours*, from Blanchot. More specifically, a curious pattern of allusion in Jabès's work explicitly links his notion of the Book to that of Blanchot. "Abandoning the book means waiting impatiently for the next book's wish to come [*Abandonner le livre, c'est se laisser suspendre au vœu du livre à venir*]" (BY 160, RL 23), remarks Jabès in *Le Retour au livre*; elsewhere, he uses the same term: "Does the book heal? That book is always to come [*Le livre est-il guérison? Il sera toujours le livre à venir*]" (YE 109, Y 152). The allusions are in fact citational, quoting as they do the title of one of Blanchot's books.[12] Along with similar passages in Jabès's work,[13] they point toward an important attribute of the Book, a vision shared by Jabès and Blanchot, the Book as process of *becoming*. This is most certainly related to Jabès's remarks about Mallarmé's construct: here, as opposed to the latter, the Book is organic and dynamic (or *will be* such, rather); it is a plurivocal, open aggregate of potentiality. It conforms thus to a model which is itself continually deferred, "a book whose words we need to cancel to let it return to its white plurality. A book which is both the promised and the denied part of the book. A book, finally, designated by a point of which we do not know if it is white in the morning and black at night, but which we could come to see as a point of the future, evolving where nothing else subsists" (LB 19, EL 24).

In the articulation of Book and book, a curious dynamic of totalization and fragmentation is at work. On one hand, the Book is a powerful totalizing figure: "The book is the unbearable totality" (CS 16); on the other hand, the book, as it is manifested in the Jabesian text, is dislocated and fragmentary. It must be so, Jabès suggests, for the book can approach the Book only tentatively, obliquely. He evokes the interdiction of representation contained in the Second Commandment to account for this: "Thou shalt not make any book in the image of the Book, for I am the only Book" (PL 50). Here the "unbearable totality" assumes another countenance, that of the jealous God. This of course rejoins an analogy often reiterated by Jabès, the *resemblance* of the writer and the Jew.[14] The writer's relation to the Book resembles the Jew's relation to God. The writing act, even as it aspires toward the Book, must eschew conventional representation, suggests Jabès. Thus the fragment, which allows the book to escape the interdiction: "The interdiction does not apply to the broken book" (PL 45).

Erecting once again a structure of transparent paradox, Jabès puts fragmentation and totalization into agonistic interplay, arguing that they are in a real sense mutually implicative and that the totality of the Book can best be glimpsed through the deliberately disjunctive character of the book:

It is in fragmentation that the immeasurable totality may be read. So it is always in relation to a purely imaginary totality that we confront the fragment. The latter figures, each time, that totality in its received, proclaimed aspect. Since it puts origin continually into question, the fragment, replacing origin, becomes itself origin of all possible, identifiable origin.

Over this fertile "deconstruction" which works in both directions—from totality to the ultimate fragment, and from the infinite fragment, annulling itself along the way in the nothingness of the preponderant fragment, in order to reconstitute through its erasure that totality—the eye is the guide, the lighthouse. (CS 53)

Here, then, is the most important function of the fragment: in its exaggerated discontinuity it suggests its contrary, eliciting a nostalgia for unity. If this is true of the fragment, it is also true of the Jabesian text for, as book succeeds book, no one book can pretend to unity. Jabès hinted at this point in differentiating his ideal of the Book from that of Mallarmé. Clearly, for Jabès, the only possible approach to the whole lies in the mutual tension—the *play*—of the disparate elements in a continually evolving aggregate: "The book plays against the book, for the unique book" (II 54).

As Jabès describes it, an important part of this process is the autonomy that the book progressively acquires. Here again is apparent the notion of oblique mimesis, for autonomy is one of the salient characteristics of the idealist construct of the Book. With each writing act, the evolving work, argues Jabès, drifts further away from its author; at a final stage, one supposes, this divorce would be complete: "The book does not need man to come into being. It does so through him" (YE 114, Y 160). The writer is in continual recession from the book, then, eventually becoming its mere thurifer.

This discourse is, of course, common in contemporary literature, where the erasure of the subject (in one form or another) has been de rigueur for thirty years and more. But it is considerably attenuated, and complicated, by a contiguous line of speculation in the Jabesian text. Even while proclaiming the dissociation of book and writer, Jabès insistently asserts the salutary value of the former for the latter. He argues that the book is the most daring human enterprise (PL 53), that it serves to keep the void at bay and helps to preserve life: "*Nier le Rien.* On that phrase, I chose to build the book. For what is living, if not the denial of nothingness?" (P 105). Both Gabriel Bounoure and Adolfo Fernandez Zoïla have remarked upon Jabès's faith in the salutary power of the book. Bounoure sees both secular and sacred parallels: the book is humankind's "chance" in Nietzsche's sense and humankind's "salvation," its Scripture.[15] Fernandez Zoïla, for his part, insists on the notion of salvation, the book as a healing labor of truth and immanence. More persuasive still is his suggestion that the book, for Jabès, is a repository of myth, principally the major myth, that of creation.[16] Creation—specifically literary creation—is equated with salvation in Jabès's work; it is a process of becoming and a guarantor of survival as he labors to build his dwelling.

Before we turn to the Jabesian book in its particulars, a few more general considerations should be noted. The first of these is the role of time in the Book. This subject, too, is curious and problematic, since the ideal toward which Jabès aspires is both solidly located in time (a mythological past) and significantly atemporal (in that it refuses conventionalist representation of time).[17] The Book is a millenary construct, the most ancient artifact of all; in this sense, it serves as the essence in which time itself is grounded: "Time begins with the book" (YE 23, Y 33). Yet the book escapes from time and from the constraints that time necessarily imposes. This aspect of Jabès's thought can best be seized on the articulative level of his texts, that level wherein they most clearly resemble the Book. "My books have neither place nor time" (DL 71), says Jabès. His statement, although of course not literally true, is highly characteristic of a certain progression in his work. In the first volume of the septology, the story of Sarah and Yukel can be located with a fair degree of precision in both space and time. Other elements in the text, however, such as the disincarnate rabbinical voices, attenuate this location. As the septology evolves, and as the story of Sarah and Yukel fades out, temporal representation recedes as well. In the works that follow the septology, this phenomenon is even more marked.

In fact, Jabès's erasure of time is concomitant to an erasure of narrative, of the story itself, and it may well be that the latter weighs more heavily on him than the former in his efforts to approach the Book. For the Book is not principally narrative; it is composed, rather, of the pure discourse of origin. Jabès says that he wishes to write in a universal language, an original language (BY 30, LY 32), implicitly stressing once again the notion of the Book as origin. Pushing the construct even further back into immemorial time is for him a process of re-memorization and purification: "The older the book the purer the face" (YE 131, E 21). Here, in the region of infinite deferral, the Book rejoins the godhead.

This leads Jabès to situate the Book within a set of equivalences, to postulate its *resemblance* to the divine: "The book is before. God is before. The universe is before. The creature is before" (II 49). The parallelism of Book and God, granted all of Jabès's ulterior discourse on the nature of the Book, seems logical enough. Both Book and God are totalizing constructs, both represent transcendence and salvation (for the writer, for humankind as a whole), and in consequence are the objects of striving, of longing; both recede infinitely before this striv-ing. Implicit within this parallelism is, once again, the analogy of the writer and the Jew.

That analogy relies on a grounding of the Book in the Jewish tradition, which Jabès achieves through the elaboration of a series of *resemblances*, and he plays upon both terms of the equivalence in turn. "Book, object of an inexhaustible quest. Is this not how the Jewish tradition sees the book?" (YE 247, A 57), questions Jabès, again returning to the notion of the quest to suggest the resemblance of the Book and the Jewish tradition. Further along in the same volume of the septology, he states categorically, "The book is Jewish" (YE 290, A 114). Elsewhere, he bases his argument of resemblance on the other term, saying for instance that the Hebrews were known as the People of the Book (LB 40, EL 48)[18] and that the story of the Jews is the story of a book (DL 50–51). In all of this speculation, the analogy of the Jew and the writer remains operative. "'The broken tablets remain the privileged model of the book,' wrote Reb Ezri, 'for each line is brokenness promised to legibility'" (LR 99): this definition of the Book is a fair characteriza-tion of Jabès's *écriture* as well; for him, writing is above all else a process of imperative (and impossible) reparation.

The Jabesian book is always beginning. For both writer and reader, the important thing is the approach, a continual hovering at the threshold of the book. This process is amply discussed in Jabès's works and is perhaps most evident in the chapter titles. The first two parts of *Le Livre des questions*, for example, are entitled "At the Threshold of the Book" and "And You Shall Be in the Book": the moment of ingress is deliberately deferred, the incipit (which is, of course, a necessary component of any book) is amplified to startling proportions, the book itself is *promised*. In *L'Ineffaçable l'inaperçu*, not only is the book deferred but also the threshold of the book: "Searching for the Threshold," "Before the Avant-Threshold," and "The Avant-Threshold" precede the part entitled "The Threshold," suggesting a wandering and a searching twice removed from the book itself. In *Elya*, this notion of double deferral is crystallized in the construct of the ground of the book, which must be approached slowly and obliquely: "Approaching the Ground of the Book."[19] In *Aely* ingress must be achieved in a tortuous itinerary through the fore-book, and the chapter titles chronicle this slow progression: "Before the Fore-Book I," "Before the Fore-Book II," "The Fore-Book I," "The Fore-Book II," "The Fore-Book III." Again, this book-before-the-book must be approached with great circumspection: *Le Livre des ressemblances* causes the reader to wait both at the "The Avant-Premier Moment of the Fore-Book" and the "Next-to-Last Moment of the Fore-Book."

The first effect of this dilatory approach is a frustration of expectation. The reader, naïvely believing to be in the book, is told that ingress is not so easily achieved: "You thought you could enter the book by the front door" (YE 177, E 91). Yet Jabès suggests that the reader's impatient waiting for the book is paralleled by that of the writer, that the writer, too, is continually searching for ingress into the book. Responding to a question posed by Marcel Cohen, Jabès suggests that the chapter titles cited above are indicative of the dilemma he faces as a writer. When he begins to write a book, he says, he is "submerged" by its material, as if a multitude of books were clamoring to be written (DL 69). He goes on to say that this material is perhaps the "absolute book" in potential form. Clearly, then, this process of approach constitutes one of the points of articulation between Book and book.

It is also a laboratory of sorts, a locus for experimentation and (inevitably) error. For if the book itself demands a fearful symmetry, a rigid and unfailing harmony, this is not true of the threshold of the book, or the book-before-the-book. There, less is at stake and a certain imperfection is permissible: "The pedestal is always banal in the case of a book" (BY 48, LY 52). The approach to the book allows for creative freedom that will progressively crumble as the book draws closer, imposing its own constraints:

The pre-text is a fertile field.
The scythe fells the sham: grain.
Naked, naked book. (DG 24, LD 41)

Within the Jabesian text, in spite of the seemingly interminable beginnings, the book is nonetheless achieved. As Jabès himself notes, this is necessary: "Thus, if there were only beginning in the book, there would never be a book" (SD 93–94). Yet the book, when one finally does accede to it, is not apotheosized, contrary to what one might expect. Rather, its dimensions, literally and figuratively, are often those of the approach that precedes it. On occasion this ratio of anticlimax is even more marked. In *Yaël*, for example, the part called "The Book" is contained in the final three pages of the text; in *Le Parcours*, the last two pages consist of a chapter entitled "Here Begins the Reading of the Book." In all this discourse, there is a latent argument, largely unvoiced but nonetheless insistent, that privileges process over product. Jabès suggests that value is not terminal but progressive, that the struggle to attain the reward is more important than the reward itself. Through all of his discourse on the book, it slowly becomes apparent that the book itself is process, dynamic rather than static, and that the book (as it is normally conceived) is far less important than the writing of the book. Along the axis of symmetry that Jabès so carefully postulates, writing as process evokes reading as process. To the reader, the prolonged beginning in the Jabesian text points toward other characteristics of that text. The deliberate and progressive "opening" functions for several critics as a sign of textual "openness." Mary Ann Caws, for example, argues that "the Jabesian book remains wide open: nonlinear, like his thought; multiple, like his inspiration; circular, like his road"; Chiara Rebellato-Libondi sees openness as resulting from the multiplicity of possible readings, from multiple means of ingress.[20] Susan Handelman suggests that Jabès's books, like the Book, are both open and closed and that this accounts for much of their power.[21]

I believe that the openness of the Jabesian text is in fact a process, a *becoming*, and that the most crucial step in that process takes place within Jabès's œuvre, as each individual book locates itself therein, embracing and interrogating those that precede it and (by implication) those that will proceed from it: "A book is always the approach to or the prolonging of another book that we have barely glimpsed" (SD 137). It is in this sense that Jabès's books demonstrate their openness most convincingly, and this phenomenon may account in large measure for the distinctiveness of his work as a whole. For, in spite of his insistence on the notion of the book, Edmond Jabès is not a writer of the book, but rather a writer of the œuvre: the importance he accords to any given book is clearly secondary when compared to that of the œuvre as a whole. Each of his books is an integer designed to take its place in the articulative play of his œuvre, his lifework. As Fernandez Zoïla has noted, "None of Jabès's books is complete, if one means by that a structure constituting a whole. All are incomplete, one engulfed in the following one, another taking root in the one preceding it. But all of them taken together constitute an *œuvre*: an *œuvre* of the All."[22]

This phenomenon is apparent in the evolution of Jabès's work, an evolution characterized by conflation and recuperation. With the publication of *Je bâtis ma demeure* in 1959, Jabès exposed the technique that he would continue to use thenceforth to build his œuvre. For that book is, precisely, a collection of books: in *Je bâtis ma demeure* Jabès grouped material from seven volumes of poetry published between 1947 and 1955, as well as other texts written from 1955 to 1957.[23] In other words, *Je bâtis ma demeure* is a cyclical work, much like the other cycles that Jabès has since elaborated. It can be viewed as a septology, like *Le Livre des questions*. The organizational scheme was imposed a posteriori; that is, Jabès brought together and thus recuperated disparate texts, imposing a new structure upon them, coercing reciprocal coherence out of them. In so doing, he undoubtedly shared the hope of all system builders that the whole would be greater than the sum of its parts.

It is a strategy that Jabès has followed consistently since that first experiment. *Le Livre des questions* began as one volume, called *Le Livre des questions*. Then, as Jabès wrote *Le Livre de Yukel* and *Le Retour au livre*, they were added to the first volume, and Jabès conceived the whole as a finished trilogy. He designates *Le Retour au livre* as the "last book" (BY 155, RL 17) and, at the end of that volume, offers a table of contents for the trilogy as a whole.[24] As *Yaël*, *Elya*, and *Aely* followed, they were not immediately integrated into the cycle. On the contrary: in *Aely* Jabès still refers to *Le Livre des questions* as a trilogy (YE 314, A 146).[25] Nonetheless, the coherence of these latter three volumes is undeniable in the progression from Yaël herself to her stillborn child, Elya, and thence to Aely, the disincarnate regard that embraces them both: the structure, in short, would seem to be that of a trilogy. It is with ·*(El, ou le dernier livre)* that *Le Livre des questions* assumes what appears to be its definitive form as a septology. The *prière d'insérer* of that volume makes this explicit: "With this work, the seventh in the series, *Le Livre des questions* draws to a close." Once again, just as in *Je bâtis ma demeure*, organization is imposed after the fact, as Jabès draws together different works and makes them cohere.

The other Jabesian cycles demonstrate a similar strategy. The procedure for *Le Livre des ressemblances* is largely analogous, although Jabès seems to have projected a trilogy from the start. Nevertheless, other similarities (*ressemblances*, precisely) in the two cycles are clear, particularly that both derive their general title from the title of the first volume in the cycle. The resemblances are such, in fact, that one wonders whether Jabès was tempted to conflate the septology and the trilogy, or rather to attach the three volumes of *Le Livre des ressemblances* to *Le Livre des questions*. Later in his work, at a time when the structure of the two cycles appeared to be definitive, he speaks strangely of the "ten" volumes of *Le Livre des questions* (PL 17). This, of course, raises a question that has been latent all along in the discussion of the articulation of individual works within cycles: how do the cycles themselves cohere within a larger ensemble, that of Jabès's œuvre? It would seem that this progressive (and hierarchical) combinatoric is one of the capital points of correspondence between the Jabesian book and the Book.

For the moment, there are two other cycles, both (as of the present writing) continuing to evolve. *Le Livre des marges*, composed of *Ça suit son cours* and *Dans la double dépendance du dit*, is the object of a curious discourse on the part of Jabès: "The texts collected here are intended to remain in the margins of my work. Their marginal character must be preserved, even emphasized, so that they may be read more freely" (CS 25). The image he chooses, that of the *margin*, is, paradoxically, one of the most central images of his writing.[26] That is, it would be difficult to choose an image that would locate a series of texts more firmly within Jabès's œuvre as a whole. *Le Livre des marges* is another project of recuperation, much like *Je bâtis ma demeure*. It is a collection of texts published elsewhere in more ephemeral form, occasional pieces, short essays, and so forth.

Finally, according to Jabès, *Le Livre des limites* will assume definitive form as a tetralogy.[27] It will group *Le Petit Livre de la subversion hors de soupçon*, *Le Livre du dialogue*, *Le Parcours*, and *Le Livre du partage*. No mention is made of the cycle in the first edition of the volumes composing it. Again, it would seem to be a case of a structure imposed a posteriori in an effort to unify seemingly disparate texts, to save them from solitary wandering, to coerce coherence.

Jabès does coerce coherence in his cycles, but in doing so he does not do violence to the individual texts. For there are elements in each of his books that facilitate this coercion, that indeed call for it, and these elements are crucial in the evolution of Jabès's œuvre as a whole. Since that evolution is principally (if not exclusively) linear, as one text succeeds and complements another, I should like to argue that its privileged figure is that of imbrication. That is, the structure of Jabès's œuvre is one of overlapping, and in each individual text one can find elements designed to support this imbricate organization. As *Le Livre de Yukel* succeeds *Le Livre des questions*, Jabès notes, "As one hand, at dawn, relieves the other, *The Book of Yukel* continues *The Book of Questions* and takes its place" (BY 13, LY 11). Three notions are evoked: relief (in the sense of relieving someone of a burden), prolongation, and substitution. The various nuances of these words converge on the idea of a work in progress, a project being passed along from one stage to the next. They emphasize the continuity of that project and seem to confirm the impression that in Jabès's writing the book is subservient to the œuvre. In like manner, when Jabès tells the reader of the third volume, *Le Retour au livre*, "This is a postface to the *Book of Yukel*" (BY 154, RL 16), the notion he wishes to convey seems to be that of prolongation. In any case, these are examples of studiously prepared textual spaces that allow for the articulation of one book with another, in a dovetail effect. The basic technique is one of autoallusion, of course. Though mostly serial (in other words, designed to link one given text to the text that precedes it), these techniques from time to time afford the imbrication of several texts. "No book is complete. Is it three times I have rewritten mine?" (BY 176, RL 40), muses Jabès, explicitly associating the first three volumes of *Le Livre des questions* in a whole, suggesting their identity.

Yaël is not directly and unequivocally associated with the three volumes preceding it, but in the *prière d'insérer* there is an implicit allusion to what at that time was the trilogy entitled *Le Livre des questions*: "Thus the book questions itself." Jabès does, however, take pains to link *Elya* to *Yaël*: "After *Yaël, Elya*. After the word in ambush for the book, a book of the refused word" (YE 149, E 50). The mutual cohesion of *Yaël, Elya,* and *Aely* is suggested in oblique manner by their titles, each being an anagram of the others. In *Aely* the three volumes are explicitly placed in association, and, moreover, Jabès points toward their affinities with the trilogy that precedes them:

> *Yukel dead.*
> *Sarah and Yaël dead.*
> *After Elya,*
> *who is Aely?*
> (YE 207, A 11)

Once again, in *Aely* there are both serial and multiple imbrications. "From here on, the book takes the place left empty by the last one" (YE 233, A 41), says Jabès, offering a vision of his work as a strictly linear process in which the privileged function is the step from one book to another, or rather the backward glance that a given book casts upon the book that precedes it. But there is also an evocation of multiplicity and a drawing together of all these books into a whole, defined figuratively by the notion of questioning, concretely by the cycle entitled *Le Livre des questions*: "My books question my books" (YE 238, A 47).
The techniques used to associate cycle with cycle are analogous to those used to imbricate the individual books within a cycle. A multiplicity of the former is to be found in *Le Livre des ressemblances*, where the *prière d'insérer* of the first volume explicitly associates that text with *Le Livre des questions*: "A new *Livre des questions*, introducing itself both as its arbitrary double and its tyrannical opposite, sees the light of day." Once again the image that subtends this passage is that of rewriting, a radical conflation of all the Jabesian books into one. This impression is reinforced by other passages in the first pages of *Le Livre des ressemblances*: "Here is a book that resembles a book—which was not, itself, a book, but rather the image of an attempt at the book" (LR 11). The *resemblance* is thus threefold: to the Jabesian book in particular, to the book in general, and to the Book in the ideal. As Jabès establishes these

resemblances, he postulates a curious, paradoxical dynamic of autonomy and dependence: "Does this book inscribe itself in their wake? Obviously, if *Le Livre des questions* had not been, this one could not have been either; but it exists on its own, as every book is the disputed prolongation or fulfillment of the book, written or to be written, to which the writer is riveted" (LR 11). Sarah and Yukel are also evoked in the first pages of *Le Livre des ressemblances*, drawing that work still closer to *Le Livre des questions* (LR 12–13). Further along, Jabès again introduces his new book, justifying it, locating it within his œuvre as he puts the key notions of *resemblance* and *questioning* into play: "The resemblance where, elsewhere, the interrogation, from work to work, was brought to its first—ultimate—term, gives us the opportunity (as is said of two colors, that they are complementary) to launch a new and close questioning, not knowing where it will lead us, except that it had already led us to the other side of the same inexhaustible book" (LR 17).

Here, then, is the problem Jabès faces. Any new book must necessarily, in its newness, cast some denial upon the work that precedes it. A fortiori, the same must be true of whole cycles of work. And yet it is just as true that any given book is stimulated and nourished by the books that precede it. It is precisely upon this seeming contradiction that Jabès builds his œuvre, playing on the notion of resemblance, which so neatly reconciles similarity and difference.

A special case of Jabès's autoreferential technique is that of autocitation; its importance in his work is considerable. Two examples will suffice here. In the final volume of the septology, Jabès quotes a passage from *Elya* and suggests that ·*(El, ou le dernier livre)* results from that passage (LB 7–8, EL 12).[28] Moreover, he says that this same phenomenon is characteristic of all his books. The passage deals with a sage and his disciple, with writing and questioning, and is thus highly appropriate to Jabès's purpose. For the theme of writing as interrogation is the principal theme of *Le Livre des questions* as a whole, and the relation of the sage to the disciple is paternal in character, furnishing a genetic model for the Jabesian book: as •(El, ou le dernier livre) was fathered by Elya, so each of his books, Jabès tells us, was engendered by another. In Le Soupçon le désert Jabès again quotes from Elya (SD 82–83).[29] The passage is heavily autoreferential; in it Jabès speaks of the circumstances of his own birth.[30] Although he was born on April 16, 1912, when his father declared his birth to the authorities he inadvertently wrote it as April 14; Jabès says that an "absence" of two days thus presided over his birth. Here again surfaces a key concept in his work, that of absence, and, once more, the idea of paternity. The principal function of techniques such as this, however, may lie elsewhere. In quoting other texts within a book, Jabès forces his reader to read those other texts (ideally, to reread), to shuttle back and forth between his various books. An analogous technique is used in L'Ineffaçable l'inaperçu, without autocitation yet more explicit still, as Jabès evokes characters from the septology: "Here everything becomes jumbled. A quick return to the preceding works proves to be indispensable" (II 102). In this manner Jabès urges his reader to consider his books as a whole and moves toward a conflation of book and book, steadily adding more cement to the walls of his dwelling.

A similar impulse is at work when he collects and retranscribes the seven prière d'insérer from Le Livre des questions in Le Livre des ressemblances (LR 19–27) and the three prière d'insérer from Le Livre des ressemblances in Le Livre des limites (PL 59–62). First and foremost, this is a project of recuperation. The status of these ten short texts as prière d'insérer was tenuous at best, paratextual (to borrow Gérard Genette's term) rather than textual. Or, to adopt a highly charged term from Jabès's lexicon, one might say that their status was marginal: his deliberate insertion of them into the main body of his work testifies once again to his paradoxical insistence upon the centrality of the margin. In a broader perspective, these retranscriptions are part of Jabès's larger strategy of imbrication; in this case the strategy is deployed on the level of the cycle rather than that of the individual text, as the entire Livre des questions is inscribed in the first volume of the cycle that follows it, Le Livre des *ressemblances*, and that cycle in turn is inscribed in the first volume of *Le Livre des limites*.

The web of resemblances that Jabès spins among his works is considerably reinforced by the titles he attributes to them. The recurrence of the word *livre* in those titles is the most obvious instance. It is especially effective on the level of the cycle, where the similarity is unavoidable: *Le Livre des* . . . "yokes" the cycles together, suggesting the mutual affinities (even, perhaps, the identity) of *questions, ressemblances, marges, limites*. Jabès plays cannily with the notion of the title and that of the book. Parts, or chapters, of individual books are occasionally themselves entitled "Le livre,"[31] which poses aporistic relations of container and contained: is the book contained in a chapter of *Yaël*, for instance, or is the book called *Yaël* subsumed in one of its chapters? This dilemma extends to the cycle in which *Yaël* participates: the chapter of *Yaël* entitled "Le livre" announces itself as closer to the Jabesian ideal than *Le Livre des questions*, whose title is more restrictive.

The example of *Le Petit Livre de la subversion hors de soupçon* is particularly interesting because its title is identical to that of a part of *Le Soupçon le désert*. "To designate two different texts by the same title: isn't this to oppose them one to the other still more strongly, arbitrarily imposing upon them a circumstantial unity?" (PL 17), asks Jabès, but in fact the function of this tactic would seem to be quite the opposite. *Le Soupçon le désert* is composed of three parts, entitled "Suspicion," "The Little Book of Subversion Out of Suspicion," and "Desert"; the middle part is thus suspended between (or framed by) two parts whose titles recapitulate that of the book that contains them. The migration of the title of this middle part, its appearance on the cover of a book, suggests an organic link between *Le Soupçon le désert* and *Le Petit Livre de la subversion hors de soupçon* and, by extension, between *Le Livre des ressemblances* and *Le Livre des limites*. The implicit model, once again, may be that of paternity; this impression is reinforced by the words *hors de*, which sound like an entry in a studbook: "out of *Soupçon*."

The iteration of the word *livre* in these various titles and the entire Jabesian combinatoric of book upon book is a crucial aspect of the straining of book toward Book. For that word in its very materiality furnishes a locus of articulation between Jabès's writings and the ideal to which he aspires. Within the word *livre* as Jabès uses it resonates both difference and identity, diachrony and synchrony. This is reflected in his remarks about his own œuvre. Or rather (more properly), the plurivocality of the word *livre* allows Jabès to present his work both as an evolving series, as "the heavy, broken chain of my writings" (YE 337, A 175), and as a coherent whole, a minute, obsessional transcription of the one book: "I still ask myself if I have really escaped from the grisaille of the first book; if I have awakened" (P 92).

One of the most striking characteristics of the Jabesian book is its resistance to generic classification. Clearly, this resistance is not a result of authorial inattention. On the contrary, it has been scrupulously cultivated by Jabès: "I dreamed of a work which would not enter into any category, fit any genre, but contain them all; a work hard to define, but defining itself precisely by this lack of definition; a work which would not answer to any name, but had donned them all" (YE 247, A 57). Jabès has been largely successful in his quest. As Mary Ann Caws notes, his work incorporates characteristics of many genres, "fiction and essay, theater and poetry, dialogue and monologue."[32]

This heterogeneity is traced on the Jabesian page, inscribed as it were in the blank spaces.[33] Visually, some pages (or parts of pages) *resemble* those of a novel, some those of a play, some those of a collection of poems. It is a question, once again, of the *margin*. A trivialist definition of poetry describes it as that genre wherein the right-hand margin is unequal. Edmond Jabès seems to play on this notion, exploiting and exploding it, for on his page none of the margins are secure. Like the letter, like the word, like the story, like, finally, the book, the margins are dislocated: they wander. Jean-Pierre Téboul notes this wandering and argues that it results in a kind of aporia: "To the tale, sometimes traversed by bits of poetry, pages of a diary, the essay is added. The writing violates and respects the law which determines belonging: aporia of the genre stripped of its specificity."[34]

In fact, Jabès's reaction against genre seems to be directed principally toward the novel. In his conversations with Marcel Cohen, he speaks of the "seizure" of the notion of the book by novelists, the popular idea that the space of the book is precisely equivalent to the space of the story it tells (DL 141). This results, argues Jabès with uncharacteristic vehemence, in an "assassination," a "strangling" of the book. According to him, the novelist refuses to accept the risk that writing ought to entail; in the hands of the novelist, the book loses its autonomy and becomes a tool, a vehicle wholly secondary to the narrative it contains. Jabès locates the novelist's sin in a lack of attentiveness to the whiteness and silence of the page: "At no moment does the novelist listen to the page, listen to its whiteness and its silence" (DL 142). All of this leads Jabès to state categorically in *Yaël*, "The day I shall write a novel I shall have left the book, have lost it" (YE 36, Y 51). Gabriel Bounoure sees in *Yaël* a stark and uncompromising reaction against the novel as genre; he calls the final portion of that book an "antinovel."[35]

Marcel Cohen suggests that Jabès's reaction goes beyond a simple refusal of traditional genres and in fact constitutes an "insurrection" within his writing (DL 69). Although *insurrection* may be too strong a term, the notion of revolt is important and can significantly illuminate Edmond Jabès's literary aesthetic. For, even though he admires and draws upon certain contemporary and noncontemporary writers, Jabès is clearly in revolt against a certain literary tradition, a tradition perhaps best defined as French belle-lettrist: "I have always been bound to the French language, but the place I feel I occupy in the literature of our country really is not, strictly speaking, a place. It is less a writer's place than the place of a book which conforms to no category. A place circumscribed then by the book and immediately claimed by the book that succeeds it" (DD 79). His remark in his conversations with Marcel Cohen is even more unconditional: "In fact, I have the feeling that I don't belong to literature" (DL 154). This radical refusal to belong may in large part account for Jabès's attitude toward genre and the consequent generic instability of his writings. Jabès is extraordinarily wary of being appropriated by the belle-lettrist tradition, wary, that is, of the trivialization that such an appropriation often entails.

From his remarks, it is clear that he views the book as the surest guarantor against any such eventuality. Through the book, the positive side of Jabès's refusal to belong becomes clear, for part of his revolt is an affirmation rather than a negation, an uncompromising valorization of marginality: "The book eludes all labels. It does not belong to any clan or class. It never follows a single vein" (YE 18, Y 28). For Jabès, the space of the margin is the space of the book, a blank space, a white space. It is the locus of creative freedom for the writer and the playground of the linguistic sign.[36]

If the characteristic color of the Jabesian book is the whiteness of the margin, its characteristic sound is silence: "This whiteness, this silence are our purest mirror" (DL 142). Here is another privileged point of articulation between Book and book, for Jabès's idealist construct is also characterized by its silence. Jabès suggests that that very silence constitutes an avenue along which the writer may approach the Book:

There is no one sacred Book, but rather books open to the silence of the sacred Book.

To write, from this silence, is to insert the Book of eternity into the mortal book of our metamorphoses. (PL 50)

This notion of silence is, of course, intimately bound up in Jabès's insistence upon the priority of the written over the oral. Once again, Jabès sees the written as being both logically and chronologically prior to the oral; the written precedes the oral in time, and its voicelessness anticipates and subsumes any voice that may resound in the book. The book itself is silent language, that is, quite simply, *writing*: "Writing: wrought crystal of silence" (YE 137, E 32).

"Wrought crystal" is a singularly appropriate image for the Jabesian book,[37] suggesting specularity and the infinite regression of figure within figure. This is the other side of Jabès's conception of his work. If he sees his writing in diachrony, as an evolving series, he also pictures it in synchrony. Jabès often says that he is writing the same book over and over again; this iterated and reiterated text finds its crystalline image in "the book within the book": "In back of the book there is the ground of the book. In back of the ground there is immense space and, hidden in this immense space, the book we are going to write in its enigmatic sequence" (YE 121, E 9).[38] Jabès relies heavily on this image,[39] and it serves him in several ways. First, it allows him elegantly to encapsulate the notion of progressive approach; thus he describes the book as a series of doors (YE 193, E 115). This process of approach is, for Jabès, characteristic of both writing and reading, in mutually reflective symmetry:

"What book do you mean?"
"I mean the book within the book."
"Is there another book hidden in what I read?"
"The book you are writing."
(BY 123, LY 129)

Both activities, reading and writing, are hermeneutic in nature, suggests Jabès. The book "hidden" within the book calls to writer and reader alike, yet it continually absconds from them, regressing even further: "And so the book would disappear in the book" (YE 125, E 13). Like God and origin, the book is infinitely deferred, allowing Jabès to concentrate on the approach, the *process* of writing and reading.[40]

More important still is the fate of the subject in this textual abyss. "I have tried, with each book, to postpone the expiration of an echo of myself" (II 97), says Jabès: the text is a mirror for the subject, but one wherein the reflected image continually recedes. Separation and alienation are thus inherent in the subject; they are necessary characteristics of the human condition. This situation in turn leads Jabès to postulate more direct, more isotopical relations between subject and book. Beyond serving as the subject's mirror, the book is actually similar to the subject; that is, they resemble each other: "An identical abyss would separate, then, man from man and the book from the book" (PL 32). Both subject and book are condemned to a certain solipsistic meditation, a specular exegesis of themselves: "Then the book is forever nailed to the book and explores without respite its grounding: its own ground?" (DG 37, LD 59).

The last steps in this progression have been implicit all along, as Jabès's discourse on subject and book changes terms once again. From *resemblance*, he moves to *identity*, but identity with a singular twist. "'I' is the book" (YE 12, Y 19), he states, echoing Rimbaud. His remark identifies subject and book but at the same time preserves a space of alterity, a buffer of difference between subject and book and (equally important) within both subject and book. Jabès finally renounces the former buffer, as he affirms unequivocally the full identity of subject and book: "The writer is his book" (DD 87).[11]

The evolution described above is a fair characterization of the itinerary of approach in Jabès's work. That itinerary is not linear, contrary to what one might expect in view of his careful nesting of book within book. For in the final analysis the relations of the various embedded figures are less than clear; "the book within the book" is an example of aporistic reduplication, to borrow Lucien Dällenbach's term.[42] In this sense, the idealist construct of the Book may perhaps not be found within the Jabesian book, but rather without. Or, as Jacques Derrida put it, "One emerges from the book only within the book, because, for Jabès, the book is not in the world, but the world is in the book."[43]

If, as Jabès himself says, the world ends up in a book (DL 121), where does the book end? That is, how can one best describe the process of emergence which Derrida alludes to? In dealing with these questions, one is necessarily led back to the notion of Jabès's texts as open works. Indeed, they are open in more than one direction for, just as each book recedes infinitely within itself, it likewise projects itself infinitely outward, toward the world. The closure techniques that Jabès uses are the surest indicators of this phenomenon. Rather than framing the book, tying it up and sealing it off, they project the book into the œuvre and, from there, into the world. The key idea, insistently recurrent in these passages, is that of survival. The survival of the book guarantees the survival of all that is to be found within it and (through the Jabesian blurring of container and contained) outside of it; the book survives, as does God, as does thought (PL 90). Since the end of the book, should it ever be reached, would entail the end of time (SD 137), the continual opening of the book is a process of resistance to the nothingness that looms beyond it: "And if the book, in its ruses and its daring, were nothing other than the lunatic resistance to the nothingness of the final page?" (P 106).

Each book points implicitly toward the book that will follow it, that will prolong it. Each book points also toward the works that precede it. It is the same with the cycles that call to each other along the grids of resemblance and eventually merge into the Jabesian œuvre. Traces of the Book's openness can be found in the book; the book, for its part, traces the opening of the Book into the world. In this reciprocality both humankind and God achieve tenuous survival: "Man does not exist. God does not exist. The world alone exists through God and man in the open book" (BY 236, RL 100). Clearly, then, even though a certain teleology is demonstrably at work in the Jabesian book, it is a paradoxical teleology at best, since it so vigorously refuses the notion of the end. Or perhaps it would be more exact to say that the end, like the origin, is continually deferred, pushed backward at the expense of constant effort and considerable guile on Jabès's part. In this light, each of his books, each cycle, and indeed his work as a whole must necessarily refuse closure, for it is only as a dynamic of becoming that the book can succor the world and the subject in the world: "The work is never complete" (PL 28).

The notion of the book as survival devolves upon the most privileged figure of the book in Jabès's work, that of the *demeure*, the dwelling. From his early writings onward, Jabès offers the *demeure* as the very image of his project. It encapsulates the project both in its aspirations and in its concrete results, for the *demeure* is both the Jabesian book in the most material sense and the ideal Book that hovers above and beyond it. It offers the writer a space of identity, shelter for the self: "The book is my home. It has always been the home of my words" (YE 273, A 91). In Jabès's universe, Jew and writer wander in a postlapsarian desert; broadening his argument, he suggests that their exile is characteristic of the human condition as a whole. Humankind has been stripped of its land, he says; it is dislocated and ungrounded. Here, precisely, is where the book, the *demeure*, comes to serve: "We had a land and a book. Our land is in the book" (BY 87, LY 93). That is, the book assumes the function of humankind's *ground*. It is far less substantial than the preexilic ground, of course; nonetheless, what substance it retains stands in stark opposition to the insubstantiality of the desert that surrounds it. This substance, however impoverished it may be, offers the only shelter available: "I was born in the book. I grew up in the book. I have never known other dwellings" (SD 112).

The book thus becomes building: "Great books! Imposing edifices [*bâtisses*]!" (LB 94, EL 109). That notion is heavily charged and, as Jabès uses it, significantly plurivocal. For, as the noun *building* in English suggests the gerund and the present participle of the verb from which it derives, so under Jabès's pen *bâtisse* points toward *bâtir*, *édifice* toward *édifier*.[44] That is, in the final analysis, the building itself may be less important to Jabès than the activity of building. This conforms to his general privileging of process over product and accounts for the fact that the *demeure*, like the book it figures, can never be finished. On the contrary, and most crucially, the *demeure* is always *building*.

This is the idea that the title of Jabès's first cycle is intended to convey: *Je bâtis ma demeure* means, quite simply, *J'écris, I write*. It is the process that constitutes the dwelling, the activity of writing the book that saves the writer, the straining toward the Book that makes it manifest in a share of ink. Edmond Jabès speaks eloquently of the despair a writer experiences in realizing that the book cannot be written, in understanding finally that he is condemned to pursue a book which he *will not write* (PL 36). Yet he is aware through all of this that the book is in fact the pursuit of the Book, a becoming that *is* already: "You dream of writing a book. The book is already written" (BY 39, LY 42).

Q....

..

figures

As soon as you place a point
you have defined the space
of the written. (DG 25, LD 42)

With all his insistence on emptiness and void, on the desert and the nonplace, Edmond Jabès nonetheless occasionally alludes to another order of space, one furnished with figure and shape. This aspect of his work testifies to a formalist impulse that, unexamined, seems incongruous: why should form assume important dimensions in this body of writing, in view of Jabès's constant iteration and valorization of the formless? Yet the attention that he accords to this concern leaves demonstrable traces on the Jabesian page, and the primacy that Jabès locates in form is indisputable: "Form makes us" (YE 169, E 80).

It is, above all, a question of space and its uses. Literary space as Edmond Jabès defines it begins with void and abyss; that is the surface upon which the writing will inscribe itself. It is a locus that may be described as distant, not only in space but also in time. In this sense, writing is a vital activity of recuperation, a laboring back toward beginnings and first things, a reverse eschatology: "Writing means having a passion for origins. It means trying to go down to the roots" (BY 159, RL 22). Jabès as always chooses his metaphors with care: an impossible distance separates the moment of writing from the moment of origin, just like the distance that separates the place of writing from the "roots" of space. This problem, like so many others in Jabès's discourse, is bound up in a rhetoric of impossibility: writing, in view of the goals it postulates for itself, is radically inadequate.

When one tries patiently to tease out the specific components of this impossibility, it becomes clear that Jabès has once again deliberately woven a tissue of obstacle and paradox. Thus space is writing's ground, the area where writing can play itself out; yet it is also the most serious obstacle that writing must overcome: "Space is in the way" (LP 95). In a similar perspective, the particular space of the book is constantly shifting in character. The manner in which Jabès describes that space is fraught with equivocation and outright contradiction. On occasion, the space of the book is void and seemingly nonfunctional: "The most heavily guarded place, the safest place of silence. Place without place or, rather, place in the nonplace of the book" (LP 119). At other moments, the book assumes materiality and subsequently projects itself into an astonishing metaphorical space: "The book takes up very little space on the table, and yet the space that it occupies is immense" (DL 50).

Consequently, any investigation of this topos must necessarily be tentative and provisional, since it will be in a real sense *groundless*. Nonetheless, it is a question that has to be posed, for the notion of literary space is for Edmond Jabès both primordial and final. The figures that the book describes as he launches it into that space are the first and last acts of writing: first, as writing constitutes a finite geometry upon the page; last, as the book plays out an infinite geometry in the literary space it furnishes. It may be argued that a principal effect of Edmond Jabès's writing is to render distinctions such as first and last, beginning and end, inoperative and absurd. Here, polarities are conflated and conjoined; more properly perhaps, writing serves to identify them: "My ambition is to trace the itinerary of the poem in lightly dotted lines. But the starting line is strangely confused with the finish line. Nothing but a chalk line, like a saber's slash in the void" (BD 164).

The geometrical analogue of such an identification is of course the circle, and the circle is one of the privileged figures in Edmond Jabès's literary space. There, a line is never straight: whether it be the chalk line alluded to in the passage quoted above or the line leading from one book to another, it always describes a curve, an arc. For a straight line implies a ground which is stable, and clearly no such ground exists in Jabès's world. It also implies definite, demonstrable progression; it is the very image of a positivist teleology, and this is another reason that Jabès refuses it. On the contrary, his lines swerve into circles, a figure that provides an antidote to the troubling certainties of the line:

A curved line is nothing other than a line frightened of its own audacity.

Reassuring image of the loop. (LP 19)

Jabès's refusal of ortholinear progression is an important part of his poetics, both thematically and formally. Itineraries in his books are not straight from point to point, but, rather, elliptical in nature. Many of the wanderings he describes can be subsumed into the notion of a *return*, graphically illustrated by the circle. Thus, just as any itinerary in Jabès is apt to retrace steps taken previously, so writing curves back upon itself: "The circle is known. Break the curve. The road doubles the road. The book consecrates the book" (BY 184, RL 48). The dynamic that Jabès erects is reflexive in character; the book and the writing that constitutes it constantly scrutinize themselves. The very nature of Jabès's discourse testifies to this circularity: iteration and autoallusion of all sorts lead the reader continually back to the capital construct of the book. In this light, the relative homogeneity of Edmond Jabès's books appears less startling, transcription being, at some point of vital necessity, retranscription.

As in writing, so in the writer. Jabès suggests that the writer's path is necessarily circular as he returns to themes and forms previously used to construct a *cycle* of work. More broadly, the cyclical nature of the book may reflect the cyclical nature of human experience and the obsession with the idea of origin and the impossible return. Here, Jabès would argue that ontogeny recapitulates phylogeny, for the individual's life can also be figured in a circle: "'One of my great fears,' said Reb Aghim, 'was to see my life round itself into a loop without being able to stop it'" (BY 185, RL 49).

Two apparently contradictory concepts seem to be at work in the figure of the circle, as Jabès deploys it: first, the idea of the infinite (or the infinitely repeatable circumference of the circle); second, that of closure (the circumscription of a given area). The latter notion rejoins a key construct in Jabès's work, that of the *limit*. For the circle limits space as well, just as it furnishes and defines space. This is undoubtedly part of its reassuring function for Jabès, since finitude and closure are far more readily conceived than the void that lies outside the circle. In this sense, too, the circle is an appropriate figure for the book: "It would mean that ring and circle are the unlimited aspect of a limit closed on its adventure" (YE 310–11, A 141). Like so many other constructs in this body of work, the idea of the limit is bound up in contradiction. On one hand, the limit postulates a constraint, a point beyond which the writer cannot go, an insurmountable (and self-imposed) obstacle. On the other, the limit marks territory as familiar, stakes a claim to it, as it were. It constitutes the material trace of the writer's passage and testifies to his construction of literary space. In this perspective, the limit is the surest guarantor of creativity: "My limits are my liberty" (LP 75).

The limit and the circle that represents it function in another manner as well. In *Ça suit son cours*, Jabès quotes a passage from Maurice Blanchot's *Le Dernier Homme*.[1] Blanchot's remark deals with the mutual affinities of end and beginning and the nature of the circle, and Jabès carefully frames the quotation with his own speculations upon the circle:

And if the circle were merely the immense happiness of the point?

"That which is the end, for you, will surely be the beginning for me. Aren't you tempted by the happiness of the circle?"
Maurice Blanchot (Le Dernier Homme)

And if the circle were merely the infinite grief of the point? (CS 69)

Jabès's tactic here is extraordinarily canny and highly illuminative of his broader technique. He has framed Blanchot's remark with his own. More precisely, he has *encircled* Blanchot's evocation of the circle, rendering the function of intertextual appropriation materially visible on the page. It is in this manner that Jabès draws the world into the book, although most other instances of this phenomenon are more subtle than this one. Clearly, however, the notion of the limit, of the boundary, is at work in this case; its function is a proprietary one, a demarcation of the territory belonging to the book. Finally, the limit is a construct that allows the author to situate himself as best he can, given the shifting ground that surrounds him:

I write in function of two limits.
On that side, there is the void.
On this side, the horror of Auschwitz. (P 95)

This passage evokes another possibility for the circle, far more somber than those I have examined thus far. If emptiness and void lie outside

131 ❖ Figures

of the circle, that which it encloses should be plenitude. Yet it is amply clear from Jabès's ulterior discourse, especially in *Le Livre des questions*, that Auschwitz signifies for him a void, the nullity of the most catastrophic event in human history. Just as a circle, graphically, is composed by a line that circumscribes an empty space, that which is enclosed by Jabès's circles, in one important sense, is death: "The void inside a circle, Aely's eye, eye of death" (YE 333, A 170).

This apparent contradiction is part of Jabès's technique of enveloping key constructs in paradox. The result is highly effective, for the circle can in turn be a figure of plenitude and of emptiness; the polarities contradict themselves, certainly, but come to complement each other in the broader field of the Jabesian book. Thus the circle encloses known, domesticated space, a *constructed* area; the book that it figures constitutes a safe locus, defined in opposition to the void that surrounds it. Conversely, the circle's limitative function is shown to be illusory because the emptiness around it is faithfully reflected by the emptiness within it; in this sense, the book, too, is a tissue of void upon void. This aspect of Jabès's meditation rejoins his image of the desert as a circle without a periphery.[2]

Pushing the image a step further in this direction, Jabès alludes to the barred circle, the null sign used by logicians and mathematicians: "Was it not a mouth propped open, round, which inspired the mathematicians to designate the void by a circle with an oblique bar?" (YE 324, A 158). In this manner, Jabès coaxes the figure of plenitude into its opposite. The strategy serves him well on the thematic level, where it functions as a material analogue of a multiplicity of other transformational constructs: the letter, the word, the story, the book.

Yet this barred, empty circle encompasses other notions as well. In a very rare example of graphic illustration, Jabès inscribes a circle on the page, traversed diagonally by the numeral one; around the circumference is written "AROUND THE VOID" (LB 51, EL 61). The text that accompanies the illustration acts as a gloss:

One: diagonal across the circle.
The void revealed across the one.
One: visibility of the circle.

In an ever-growing sea,
O survival of the grain of salt.

Once again, the circle is empty at the very moment when it would seem, graphically, to be the fullest. The numeral one, which crosses it, does not guarantee plenitude; on the contrary, it renders plenitude impossible. The void, too, has undergone a transformation in this instance. Its locus has been radically shifted with regard to the circle: from *outside*, it has migrated *inside*, constituting a stark reversal of normative, intuitive topography. It is the number one, figure of unity and fullness, that renders the void visible, suggests Jabès, but that numeral is the object of an important transformation signaled by the capitalization in the third line of the accompanying text. The one, in effect, becomes the One, metaphor upon metaphor, yet another image of the elusive God that traverses the Jabesian book.

If God is the slash that renders the circle null, he is also the circle itself: "And if God were the smallest circle?" (SD 37). The image, for Jabès, is extraordinarily efficient: here, the circle constitutes perfection and eternity, yet it is the vital image of the void; it is obvious in form and easily apprehended, but it is impenetrable; it is all-encompassing, yet that which it circumscribes is emptiness. Granted the convergence of their respective attributes, the identification of God and the circle is inevitable. Elsewhere, in a characteristic accretion of figures, Jabès says: " 'This circle,' he said, 'which the blotter has made into a point invaded by night, is God' " (LB 8, EL 12). The technique he employs here is covert, oblique: in fact, this passage, from ·*(El, ou le dernier livre)*, is a direct quotation from *Elya*.[3] Jabès carefully notes this borrowing and suggests that the passage from *Elya* may have inspired ·*(El, ou le dernier livre)*. More precisely, autocitation as a literary device can be graphically illustrated as circular; Jabès's use of that technique in ·*(El, ou le dernier livre)* is most deliberate: the latter book is, after all, the seventh volume in the *Livre des questions* septology and constitutes one of the points where Jabès's writing comes full circle.

The circle figures God, then, but it also (and more immediately) figures the œuvre. This is implicit in the notion of the *return*, which is so insistent in Jabès's work. Gabriel Bounoure was the first to note the circularity of the first three volumes of *Le Livre des questions*, which Jabès then conceived of as a finished trilogy:

> *Edmond Jabès's three great books are joined in the unity of a circular composition. The work draws to a close in fact in a return to the book. The first volume showed the negative power of language, annihilating things in their existence. It was as if the verb of the lone I must perish from narrowness like the I itself. Then, in the second volume, after the revelation of love, the horror of history and of Evil were seen to drown individual destinies, a negativity more violent than that which plays treacherously in the ideality of the word. Finally, the poet came back to the book, moving from the con to the pro, traveling backwards, as if writing were charged with an original energy capable of overcoming so many denials.[4]*

This circularity is inscribed on the first three volumes of *Le Livre des questions*, both thematically and structurally, but it is particularly evident in *Le Retour au livre*, whose very title evokes the circular nature of the return and announces the cyclical character of the œuvre:

> *Three questions*
> *charmed the book,*
> *three questions*
> *will finish it.*
> *Whatever ends*
> *began three times.*
> *The book is three.*
> *The world is three.*
> *And for man, God*
> *is three replies.*
> (BY 210, RL 75)

Each of the major cycles in Edmond Jabès's work involves this sort of return. More generally, it can be said that each individual book is itself circular, the end clearly rejoining the beginning. In close analysis, moreover, it becomes apparent that the circle is the characteristic *local* structure within each book, as echoes and resonances, queries and interrogations play themselves out. That is, at every level of Jabès's writing, from the sentence to the œuvre, the reader is confronted by this recurrent figure; it is thus by a natural movement that Jabès *returns* to it when alluding to his work as a whole: "A work round like the world where All moves towards All and Nothing towards Nothing in its legitimate will to be" (YE 156, E 60).

Gabriel Bounoure sees in this phenomenon a dynamic of questioning; he suggests that the tension between the circle and its center is interrogative in character.[5] The notion of the center, however, is highly problematic in this body of work, as we shall see. Adolfo Fernandez Zoïla, for instance, envisions the Jabesian text as a spiral, a continual process of distanciation from the center.[6] Rosmarie Waldrop, too, argues that Jabès's work describes a spiral, an interrogation that progresses toward openness rather than closure.[7] In a very important sense, however, Bounoure's suggestion offers a crucial insight, for the figure of the circle is consistently opposed to the other transcendent figure in Edmond Jabès's writing, the *point*. Whether the latter be defined as the *center* or not, the tension prevailing between the circle and the point (the play of the two, precisely) is the source of much aesthetic efficacy in the Jabesian text.

Curiously enough, in view of the symmetrical relations prevailing elsewhere, Jabès defines the point as emanating from the circle: "Like the smallest circle—a new center—that is how I defined the point in *Le Livre des questions*" (DD 17). When the origin of the point is in question, it is once again a matter of transformation, the transformation of the circle into the point: "Here, yesterday's circle has shrunk to a point, the questioning of the circle to that of the point" (LB 8, EL 12).

It is in •*(El, ou le dernier livre)* that Jabès's meditation on the point becomes most intense,[8] and there the transformation of circle into point is very clear: the seventh volume of *Le Livre des questions* closes the cycle, and in doing so defines a sort of *point final*. As the end of the septology rejoins and recapitulates the beginning, Jabès questions the idea of movement, of progression; the point appropriates, consequently, the function of the circle as figure of the book. ·(*El, ou le dernier livre*) constitutes, then, the moment in Jabès's writing when the point comes into its own and assumes, paradoxically enough, dimension. The point, after all, serves as the title of that book; the rest is parenthetical, secondary, and incidental. As title, the point dominates every page of the book, for it is quite naturally inscribed at the top center of each page, as a running head. A glance at the table of contents shows a series of ten points, with corresponding numbers in both roman and arabic numerals: the chapter titles are points, also.

The tension that Jabès exploits here is played out between two different sorts of semiotics, verbal and nonverbal. *Le Livre des questions* puts language on trial, in a manner progressively more stringent; in the "last book" this line of interrogation culminates in the point. The latter is not so much averbal as antiverbal. It is the "point of space unmarked by any letter" (LB 16, EL 20), and it defines the end of the book, as well as the end of language. Its *marginal* character is strongly marked: minimal manifestation of ink on the page, it stands in stark opposition to the words that surround it, finally subsuming them in the privileged role it plays in the dynamic of finality. Thus once again does Jabès render the marginal central. Like the marble Yukel played with as a child, the point is "out of the game, but its innermost stake" (LB 3, EL 7).

The further transformations of this figure are strictly analogous to those undergone by the circle, by the book, and by other key constructs in Jabès's writing. Just as any given circle implies all other circles (since all circles are identical in form), and every circle encloses and projects an infinity of concentric circles; just as Jabès directs the reader of every book to both the Book and the book-within-the-book; so too does the point engender other points in an infinitely regressing perspective:

A point
drowned
in a point.
(LB 33, EL 39)

In similar fashion, fullness gives way to emptiness. Experimenting in pointillism, Jabès traces the word *NUL* in black points on a white background; underneath, he writes *L'UN* in white points on black (LB 52–53, EL 63), expressing thus a relation of reciprocity that recalls the play of plenitude and void in the circle. As a result of this parallelism, four key terms, the circle, the point, plenitude, and void, are placed into an agonistic dynamic that is intended to figure the Jabesian book in all its apparently contradictory aspects: if the book is closed, it is also open; if the book is motionless, it is nonetheless impossibly unstable; its very fullness is the most eloquent testimony to the emptiness within it.

Among its other transformations, the point often becomes incarnate, chiefly in the form of an eye. Thus, according to Jabès, words must be reduced to points (CS 68), and one must think of them as eyes that contemplate the reader from the page (SD 15). Similarly, Jabès calls Aely "eye of All and of Nothing" (LR 25); Aely can be defined in fact only as this disincarnate *regard*, shorn of any other corporality:

who is Aely? He is oblivion, I said. Oblivion of the scarred, disemboweled woman crushed by her stillborn child. Oblivion of the world, oblivion of life and the void.
The eye of all that has not been.
(YE 207, A 11)

The *regard* of Aely, like that of the book and the words that compose it, becomes a sort of law for Jabès. He speculates indeed on the literal affinities of the words *oeil* and *loi* (YE 205–6, A 9–10) and later postulates a condition of reading strongly reminiscent of the *lex talionis*:

An eye for an eye,
the look insists.
(YE 266, A 82)

The eye in other instances undergoes further transformation, as when it comes to figure other parts of the human anatomy. In some cases, one can trace a transformation which is at least triple, as point gives way to eye, which in turn becomes (for instance) a vagina: "Your sex, woman, is the empty eye of death" (YE 266, A 81). For Jabès, the point and its first anatomical analogue, the eye, are intimately bound up in a dynamic of sexuality and reproduction: "An eye remembers and awakens my memory. An eye like a sheath for the one—primordial figure, Unity, Totality of God—to slide in, a rod in attack. O Marriage-wound" (YE 217, A 25). The passage strongly resembles the image in •*(El, ou le dernier livre)* where the numeral one traverses the circle, rendering it void (LB 51, EL 61); there, too, the one becomes the One. In the passage at hand, however, Jabès brings together a multiplicity of key images, grouped around the figure of the point. The notion that resonates most insistently in the passage is that of unicity: the point is one, God is one, the number is first and original, female and male achieve unity in the sexual act.

If the point demonstrably serves as a figure of female sexuality, Jabès nonetheless also associates it with the male: "Point. Drop of sperm" (LB 61, EL 71). Although this double association may seem paradoxical on first consideration, its importance lies in the reconciliation and identification of opposites. That is, the point defines the locus where male and female conjoin; what Jabès is *pointing* toward here is the act of conception, of creation. The implications of such imagery are obviously very broad indeed. But I think that their most immediate import involves writing and its modes and possibilities; the point, like the circle, is a metaphor whose principal tenor is the Jabesian book. In such a light, the conflation of male and female in the figure of the point can be seen to be very appropriate indeed, for the ritual that Jabès is acting out on the page through this imagery is the process of literary creation: "From this point we have conceived the book" (LB 103, EL 121).

Conception as a metaphor functions, of course, as part of the more ample discourse on origin that runs through Jabès's writing. Although Jabès defines the point as emanating from the circle, the point for him shares the originary status of the latter. It is single and alone; just as the number one is the "primordial" numeral, so the point is first in the order of things: "In the beginning was the point" (P 28). The relations of the point and the word, or the *logos*, are obvious in this passage, as Jabès paraphrases the beginning of John's gospel.

The point is thus triply associated with the divine: first obliquely, through the intermediary of the circle, and granted the series of equivalences (or resemblances, more appropriately) that Jabès elaborates between the point and the circle; next, through the word, whose relations to the divine are clear both in Jabès's imagery and in that of the biblical intertext. Finally, the point is related directly and explicitly to the divine, as Jabès, quoting the cabala, declares one of his sources for the point in the final volume of *Le Livre des questions*: "When God, *El*, wanted to reveal Himself, He appeared as a point" (LB 3, EL 7). The point is the originary locus of the godhead, then, but it is also the antiverbal sign that is the unpronounceable name of God.[9] Considering that Jabès chose to use the point as the title of his book, the identification with God entails metaliterary consequences that are extraordinarily far-reaching. God becomes present, on one level at any rate, both in language and in the book. The point as it manifests itself in Hebrew diacritics, suggests Jabès, serves as the guarantor of God's presence and consequently assures the legibility of the text: " 'God's point of view,' he said, 'is a *point*. Hebrew made a vowel out of it, so that, all writing having finally become visible (thanks to the point), in each word, God's point of view might be read'" (LP 92).[10] Here once again Jabès introduces the reader to the emblazonment of book within book, for the material point is the analogue of any number of immaterial, ideal points, just as the book reflects the impossibly distant image of the Book: "God is the incandescent point facing the dark point of the written page. For to man's book of nights corresponds God's blinding book of light" (BY 21, LY 21).

Like God, then, the point is primordial, both first and original. It is also, however (again like God), the last of things, the final point in Jabès's eschatological itinerary. It is, after all, the title of the "last book":

Ah, the last book would be nothing other, perhaps, than the trace of a book through which God would wish Himself visible.

Thus the point. (LR 90)

The point as title defines the originary locus of the book, and, as the closing period, it defines the end as well: "'Do you know that the final period [*point final*] of the book is an eye,' he said, 'and without lid?'" (YE 203, A 7). In the case of the circle, such an apparent opposition is easily resolved, beginning and end each becoming the other in the infinity of circumference. In his interrogation of the point, Jabès reconciles first and last in an allusion to Judaic tradition; he notes that the Hebrews compared the present to a point, seeing in it both the end of the past and the beginning of the future (DD 7). The image is rich and very well suited to Jabès's purposes. For the present is comparable to a point in that neither possesses extension (in time, in space). The present, moreover, is at the middle of things; continually hovering between past and future, it defines the *center* of experience.

When Jabès redefines the point as the center of the circle, he accomplishes the cardinal gesture in his figuration of literary space. Therein he assembles and associates many key constructs and images that wander elsewhere through his work. In other words, the center serves Jabès as a privileged locus of *resemblance*:

The center is a well.

The center is a scream, an open wound, a key.

"Do not bet on calming the waves," said Reb Fayah. "The sea holds a grudge."

"Where is the center?" howled Reb Madiés. "The disowned water lets the falcon pursue his prey."

The center is perhaps a shift in the question.

*No center [*point de centre*] where no circle possible.* (BY 193, RL 57)

The images in this passage together constitute a catalog of key Jabesian metaphor. The well is the *puits* or, to use another expression, the *point d'eau*, the oasis. It stands alone in the desert and functions as the antithesis of the desert. Like the minimal share of ink on the page that is the point, it stands in opposition to all that surrounds it: black against white, wet and life-giving against dry and desiccated, plenitude against emptiness. The well is also the abyss; as such, it is a figure of the book in its own right, a book wherein real ingress is constantly deferred. The cry is Sarah's cry, the wail that resonates throughout *Le Livre des questions* and beyond. Like the point, it is not so much averbal as antiverbal; it is a final reaction against language and the world that language so inadequately represents. It is the sign of the catastrophic wound that the world inflicts on the subject. Consequently, as Jabès makes amply clear elsewhere, it is the very sound of the book, a key to possible and impossible approach. When Reb Madiés, the imaginary rabbi, seeks the center, he recapitulates a quest engaged upon by Jabès himself as author, as well as by anyone who reads Jabès's work in a serious manner: it is a *question*, on one hand, of testing out the limits and potentialities of writing; on the other hand, of elaborating strategies and logics through which legibility appears on the horizon of possibility. The center is after all the only pertinent locus, the only place with any definition in a topography which is otherwise uncharted and shifting. It is the *point* toward which all desire in this body of work strains: that of an imaginary rabbi, that of Edmond Jabès, that of Sarah and Yukel, of Yaël, Elya, and Aely, that of the reader. Characteristically, Jabès suggests that the center is "perhaps" the displacement of the question. The eternal "perhaps" of the Jabesian nonassertion is inherently destabilizing; it is *itself* interrogation and thus displacement; it puts radically into question all the terms that encircle it. If there is no center (*point de centre*, in the original) where the circle is impossible, it is largely because of this displacement. To imagine a center without a circle is akin to imagining a circle without a periphery; and yet, as we have seen, this is precisely what Jabès asks of his reader,[11] and it is by no means the broadest leap of faith that the reader is called upon to make.

Locating the center is one of the principal tasks that the Jabesian text sets forth for the reader. Jabès himself suggests that it may be the final task: "The last obstacle, the ultimate border is (who can be sure?) the center" (BY 193, RL 58). It is as if Jabès had deliberately erected a hierarchy of obstacles in the text, arranged in increasing order of difficulty. In this sense, each obstacle, once it is successfully overcome, disassembled, or skirted, affords another level of ingress into the text. The movement described in such a model of reading is that of a straining toward the center, precisely, and the center itself is the last barrier between reader and book: "The center is threshold" (BY 194, RL 58).

In another perspective, Jabès defines the center somewhat differently, furnishing it with other attributes. He suggests in one instance that the act of writing is, by its very nature, always central: "The hand writes between points. Along with the word, it is forever center" (LB 21, EL 26). If this be the case, the shifting of the center that Jabès alludes to can be explained more readily, for the center would follow the dynamic itinerary of the writing hand as it moves across the page and through the book.[12] A successful reading would attempt to approximate or reconstruct this motion as faithfully as possible. Jabès avoids the problem of intentionality (or could claim to avoid it, at least) through the synecdochal figure of the writing hand, an instrument that functions independently of the author's will. Still, Jabès is careful to situate questioning at the center of his concerns. He compares Mallarmé's Book and the Bible, suggesting that they are polar opposites. The biblical texts follow no coherent structural scheme; that is, none of them was written with a vision of the whole into which it was to be interpolated. Yet Jabès argues that the Bible comes closer to the ideal of the Book as he conceives of it, granted its openness and its process of questioning: "The questioning of the book, which is at the center of my work, made me realize that, afterwards. Each writer dreams of writing the Book. Every work testifies to that one desire" (DL 120). For Jabès, then, questioning and the aspiration toward the Book that engenders it are irrefutably *central*.

The description of interrogation as central, the postulation of the center as the necessary locus of the act of writing, would seem to entail consequences that are, on the face of it, starkly incongruous with the rest of Jabès's discourse on writing in general and on his own project in particular. For if the center is security, then writing is itself safe; if the center is the last point, then writing has reached the end and has no further to go. But Jabès, conscious of this dilemma, suggests that the writer attains the center only to be expelled from it: "Here more than anywhere else, I am at the center of health, of the solid word. But precisely by being so robust this word drives me away" (BY 30, LY 31). In this sense, the center defines a point of exile and rupture rather than a place of salvation for writer and book; it is a paradise from which one is continually driven away. The center becomes, then, a place of distance rather than proximity. Richard Stamelman has argued that the rupture at the center of existence is reflected in language, and he evokes the metaphor of the Diaspora to characterize the textual consequences of such distanciation: "Diaspora is the condition of all writing. Because the past can never be recovered in its full intensity and the immediacy of experience can never be translated into words, and because objects of longing forever elude the grasp of desire and the self is so plural and protean as to be always different from the definition words may give it, language is in a state of profound and irreversible exile: a rootlessness that reflects the essential separation and distance at the center of being."[13]

One accedes to the center only to find that the conditions of existence pertaining elsewhere, instability and displacement, are not resolved therein, but on the contrary, are amplified. Creation as a central activity thus necessarily entails destruction: "The center is failure. The Creator is rejected from His creation. Splendor of the universe. Man destroys himself as he creates" (BY 194, RL 58). As Jabès once again evokes the analogy of God and writer, he suggests that both are doomed to failure and exile. For God can be located in the center: "God is the all-embracing center" (YE 43, Y 59); yet the immediate and inevitable consequence of this is a radical *dislocation*.

The center in this light represents for Jabès the very figure of the impossible in writing and in existence; it becomes a place of nostalgic longing and grief: "The center is mourning" (BY 194, RL 59). This allows him to articulate yet another field of metaphor wherein the center as vehicle comes to correspond to a very particular tenor. In a dynamic of interrogation, Jabès once again locates the center:

"Where is the center?"
"Under the cinders."
(BY 194, RL 59)

Ash here figures the end of life, the biblical *memento mori*; like Job, the writer and his remembrances have turned to ash.[14] It is also the material residue of destruction and death; loss objectified, it is the very stuff of grief, of mourning. As center, it is also the point; as the title of ·*(El, ou le dernier livre)*, it is the locus of finality, evoking all other last things: "A point so small, and yet it holds the ashes of all other points" (LB 4, EL 9). When Jabès brings his metaphor more and more sharply into focus, it becomes clear that the ash is most pertinently the ash of the Holocaust and that the status of that event in human experience is central: "The young man saw his mother and father caught in the trap, become the festering middle [*centre*] of a raid, the burden of a humbled rose, and disappear with its scent" (BY 197, RL 63). At the center, then, there is no salvation, but rather arbitrary persecution, cruelty, and death. In the image of the camps as center, Jabès announces the most sober and fundamental line of questioning in his work: "Aside from challenging God, the center formed by the many extermination camps left the Jews—chosen people of the center—grappling with the interrogations of their race" (BY 198, RL 63). Locus of origin and writing, creation and divinity, the center is also (and perhaps *consequently*) the crucial arena of catastrophe. It is a scene of immolation and rupture; a ground that continually demonstrates the impossibility of any sort of grounding; a place, paradoxically but most precisely, of displacement.

Thus understood, the center in Jabès's work exists merely to deny its own existence: it describes a movement that is, finally, eccentric. Maurice Blanchot was the first of Jabès's critics to note this phenomenon and comment on it: "The two experiences, that of Judaism and that of writing, at once joined and separate, which Edmond Jabès expresses and affirms, the one through the other, but also through the patience and generosity of his double vocation, have their common origin in the ambiguity of this rupture which, even in its explosion, reveals the center (essence, unity), while leaving it intact, but which is perhaps also the explosion of the center, the eccentric point which is center only in the shattering of its explosion."[15]

This eccentric movement represents, I believe, the key dynamic of the Jabesian text. Moreover, the decentered circle seems to be the one figure in Jabès's work upon which his critics unanimously agree. Gabriel Bounoure, speaking of *Yaël*, states quite simply and directly, "the center becomes decentered."[16] He argues that *Le Livre des questions* proposes no center where questioning could be assembled and eventually resolved; the poetic force of the book is in wandering that recapitulates the Diaspora.[17] Bounoure's notion of the mutual interrogation of the circle and the center alluded to earlier again appears most pertinent. In *Le Livre du dialogue*, Jabès offers the image of the center and the circle radically divorced one from the other, both wandering, each questioning the other in the nostalgia of impossible union:

One said: "I am a point. Ah, one day I should like to discover the circle whose center I must be: my world."

The other said: "I am a circle. Ah, one day I should like to discover the center which makes sense of the adventure of the line." (DG 11, LD 21–22)

Joseph Guglielmi insists on the idea of the rupture, of the shattering of language and structure. He argues that this event is the cause of the decentering in Jabès's work and that the event itself becomes subject.[18] The decentered composition of the Jabesian text, Guglielmi suggests, entails two principal effects. First, the discourse assumes progressively more distance from its origins,[19] launching itself into the void; second, it anticipates and foils commentary more and more definitively. In this fashion Guglielmi postulates a relation of the book to its "before" and "after" that is characterized by ever more distance. The figure that he describes (but never directly and unequivocally enuciates) is that of the spiral, which seems in many instances a fair representation of Edmond Jabès's writing: "Distance is the dizziness of the curve. But what center, one day, will be able to hold its circle?" (CS 61).

Edith Dahan alludes, like Blanchot and Guglielmi, to explosion and rupture in the Jabesian book. The object of this destructive process, she believes, is language and the stable world it supposedly reflects and guarantees: "Jabesian writing asserts itself as procedure and action, pulverizing the plenum of the subject, the triumphant and totalitarian homogeneity of meaning, the homological relation of the world to its language."[20] She attributes an "extraordinary plastic force" to this body of work that allows it to uproot itself from all places of origin and end; allows it, that is, to refuse all and any attempt at domestication. The source of this force, she argues, lies in the structure of the Jabesian book, disseminated in fragments, plural, multiple, and varied, and thus generically unclassifiable; in the syntax that Jabès practices, classical and balanced, which dissimulates explosive effects; and in the initial project begun with *Le Livre des questions*, a project based on interrogation and a Heraclitean vision of universal motion.[21]

Richard Stamelman, too, cites the fragmentation and multiplicity of form of the Jabesian text, along with the "rhetoric of discontinuity" that they erect, as key sources of its decenteredness.[22] He suggests that there is no opposition between the text and the world on this level because both are unstable and constantly shifting; the wandering of the text reflects the nomadic character of the human condition. Whence the importance of the desert as image for Jabès: it is the place of the nonplace, argues Stamelman, the outside, the margin, the locus of exile. There, existence is colored by loss. The desert has no presence, no *here*, no *now*: it lacks a center.[23] It is, briefly put, the proper terrain of the book, of experience, and of the writing that attempts to come to terms with the latter.

Adolfo Fernandez Zoïla locates the problem of decentering historically, arguing that if it was inaugurated in modern thought by Galileo, it was not until the beginning of the twentieth century that the idea came into its own. He cites the influence of Debussy and Mahler in music; that of Picasso, Picabia, Klee, Kandinsky, and Mondrian in painting; that of Nietzsche, Hölderlin, Mallarmé, Joyce, Dada, and surrealism in literature. Pursuing the parallels between music, painting, and literature upon which his thesis is grounded, Fernandez Zoïla suggests that, until recently, literature lagged somewhat behind in the explosion of abstraction, that literature had not produced a Stockhausen or a Barnett Newman; it was Edmond Jabès, he says, who came to fill this gap.[24] His argument is curious, for what he is describing is a dynamic by which the avant-garde becomes canonical, by which, precisely, the marginal becomes central. Such a vision would seem to contradict his definition of the decentering effect as one of radical and irrecuperable marginalization.[25] On the face of it, moreover, to position Jabès at the end point of a long procession of precursors in the history of literature is, I think, to adopt the one figure that seems most irrevocably banished from his writing, the line, and to trivialize the very arguments that his work puts forward most eloquently, most forcefully: the book, like experience, tends continually to escape from circumscription; it is fragmentary and ephemeral; it is apprehended only to be lost. This is why the center is always displaced, why the locus of thought and action is always marginal: "Center of multiple representation, of the circle and its metamorphosis *in* the circle, or of the circle and its metamorphosis *after* the circle, the center—which is a knot of truth—is, each time, elsewhere" (CS 31).

Jacques Derrida's critique of the center as construct is highly illuminative of Jabès's strategy. Derrida argues that the center has always been used to neutralize structure. It stands for presence and stable origin; its role is to organize the structure, to order and balance it. More important, however, the center functions to constrain the structure, to limit or circumscribe its play. In this manner, what play remains takes place on a rigidly defined, circumscribed ground; it is static and codified. That dynamic, in short, is the very opposite of what we commonly regard as *play*.[26] Derrida suggests that cultural history in the West can be seen as an impossible and repeated evocation of the center: "If this is so, the entire history of the concept of structure, before the rupture of which we are speaking, must be thought of as a series of substitutions of center for center, as a linked chain of determinations of the center. Successively, and in a regulated fashion, the center receives different forms or names. The history of metaphysics, like the history of the West, is the history of these metaphors and metonymies."[27] Jabès describes a similar repeated substitution, with the nuance of the *eccentric* center, testimony to its status as an impoverished, inadequate construct, the product of an overwhelming nostalgia for origin and stability: "Circle after circle, the center, always decentered, created, in order to reassure itself perhaps, an original fixed center" (DL 134).

The rupture that Derrida alludes to is the moment when structure, and with it the notion of the center, is finally put into question. From that point forward, he argues, it became necessary to think of the center not as a place but rather as a function, or to think that there was no center. This is analogous to the "shattering," the "explosion" that other readers of Jabès evoke. Though that event may be catastrophic for certain codified systems of thought, its local consequences for any given structure are wholesome and liberating. As Derrida puts it, "The absence of the transcendental signified extends the domain and the play of signification infinitely."[28] Edmond Jabès recognizes the force of such a metaphysics and exploits it, as, having repeatedly used the center as a figure of his own work, he finally and unequivocally abstracts it from figuration: "The center does not exist. It is the point around which an eccentric discourse revolves, around which a questioning develops. It is the point of no return" (DD 79).

It is an astonishing gesture on Jabès's part, which both negates and affirms. If it erases any possibility of stable meaning, it nonetheless invests the book with an endless potential of signification; if it denies the existence of origin, it also proposes the margin as the real theater of experience; if it sternly evacuates the answer from the realm of discourse, it offers in its place the question. It is a point of no return but also a vantage point from which Jabès can survey his work:

Today, in point of fact, I see these books as so many unclosed circles forming, if one approaches them in their continuity, a spiral with an eccentric center. The center of this spiral is a circle reduced to a point in space. This visible point—materialized in the title of the seventh Livre des questions by a red point—is both the beginning and the end of these volumes. It reminds us that "When God wanted to reveal Himself, He appeared as a point." This red point on the cover symbolizes for me the erasure of the book, the erasure of God, the failure of language, and also the origin of all writing, for, after all, it is because of a lack that we decide to write, that we speak. This point is, as it were, the visibility of that lack.

Remember too that to put pen to a blank page is invariably to mark space with a point. (DL 83)

The figure is not plenitude, then, but emptiness; it marks the book and is marked by it. The center has no possible pertinence in a corpus scarred to this extent by loss. Having been radically rethought, the structure has passed around the center, playing freely, skirting the center and rendering it inoperative, unable to govern or constrain. This is the way Jabès constructs his literary space: elliptically, through inscription but also through erasure, making absence manifest on the page:

A circle
and in the circle another
circle
and in the new circle still
another circle
and so on till
the last: a forceful
point,
then an invisible point
unbelievably present,
majestically absent.
A woman and a word.
A woman turning
around a world turning
slowly, faster,
unbelievably fast
till they are but
one circle in the space that spawned them
pursuing a smaller
and ever smaller,
grotesquely tiny circle.
A hole. An empty socket.
An eye of night.
A shattered eyeball.
And then? You look.

You plunge.
Is this what is called unity:
a circle undone?
A circular scream,
step,
and avowal?
(YE 11–12, Y 18–19)

Traveling around the periphery of Edmond Jabès's work, the first problem one encounters is that of ingress. Curiously and without forewarning, the terms of the problem change in the course of that itinerary: what one seeks now is issue. But one seeks it reluctantly, and is cheered to find that it seems as impossibly distant as its opposite. One doesn't wish for the Jabesian book to end. One doesn't wish for reading to end. And, in a sense, they do not:

Circular work; you must tackle my work in its circles.
And each of them will demand a new reading. (YE 143, E 41)

n o t e s

1. LEGIBILITY

1. On writing and the Holocaust in Jabès's work, see the introduction in Eric Gould, ed., *The Sin of the Book* (Lincoln: University of Nebraska Press, 1985), esp. xv, xvii, xxiii; and, in the same volume, Berel Lang, "Writing-the-Holocaust: Jabès and the Measure of History," 192–206. See also Raymond Federman, "Displaced Person: The Jew / The

Wanderer / The Writer," *Denver Quarterly* 19, no. 1 (1984): 85–100. I shall discuss this problem at greater length in Chapter 4.

2. Marcel Cohen, "Lorsqu'une oeuvre . . . ," *Les Cahiers Obsidiane* 5 (1982): 9.

3. Sydney Lévy, "The Question of Absence," in Gould, ed., *Sin*, 155–56.

4. Joseph Guglielmi, *La Ressemblance impossible: Edmond Jabès* (Paris: Les Editeurs Français Réunis, 1978), 171.

5. See Henri Raczymow, "Qui est Edmond Jabès?" *Les Cahiers Obsidiane* 5 (1982): 158–67.

6. Susan Handelman, " 'Torments of an Ancient Word': Edmond Jabès and the Rabbinic Tradition," in Gould, ed., *Sin*, 55–91, esp. 64–65.

7. For a more ample discussion of this notion and Jabès's own exploration of his "Judaism after God," see DL 87–101.

8. See, for example, "Lettre à Gabriel," BY 131–34, LY 137–41; "Lettre à M.C.," R 81–84; "L'Inconditionnel (Maurice Blanchot)," CS 87–108; "L'Inconditionnel, II (Maurice Blanchot)," DD 101–3; "Lettre à Jacques Derrida sur LA QUESTION DU LIVRE," CS 41–61.

9. Francis Wybrands, "La Rumeur, le désastre," *Les Cahiers Obsidiane* 5 (1982): 101.

10. See, for instance, LB 64, EL 74.

11. Jacques Derrida, "Edmond Jabès and the Question of the Book," in *Writing and Difference*, trans. Alan Bass (Chicago: University of Chicago Press, 1978), 77.

12. Guglielmi, *Ressemblance*, 169–70.

13. Lévy, "Question of Absence," 158.

14. Chiara Rebellato-Libondi, "Rien ne se crée, rien ne se perd," trans. Arlette Jabès, *Les Cahiers Obsidiane* 5 (1982): 111.

15. See Cohen, "Lorsqu'une oeuvre . . . ," 9: "Every real reader of Jabès bears the stigmata of a cataclysm, without which he remains a stranger to the work."

16. See Gérard Macé, "La Poésie par défaut," in Gabriel Bounoure, *Ed-*

mond Jabès: La demeure et le livre (Montpellier: Fata Morgana, 1984), 12.

17. On the topos of the mirror and its structural function in contemporary literature, see Lucien Dällenbach's remarkable *Le Récit spéculaire: Essai sur la mise en abyme* (Paris: Seuil, 1977).

18. See Maurice Blanchot, "L'Interruption," *Nouvelle Revue Française* 137 (1964): 869–81. This essay was translated into English by Rosmarie Waldrop and Paul Auster as "Interruptions," in Gould, ed., *Sin*, 43–54.

19. Blanchot, "Interruptions," 44.

20. See Roland Barthes, *S/Z* (Paris: Seuil, 1970), esp. 16–18.

21. Edmond Jabès, "The Question of Displacement into the Lawfulness of the Book," trans. Rosmarie Waldrop, in Gould, ed., *Sin*, 238.

2. THE LETTER

1. See Rosmarie Waldrop, "Mirrors and Paradoxes," in Gould, ed., *Sin*, 133–46.

2. See, for instance, Georges Perec, *La Disparition* (Paris: Denoël, 1969), *Les Revenentes* (Paris: Julliard, 1972), *Alphabets* (Paris: Galilée, 1976), *La Clôture et autres poèmes* (Paris: Hachette, 1980); Oulipo, *La Littérature potentielle: Créations, recréations, récréations* (Paris: Gallimard, 1973), *Atlas de littérature potentielle* (Paris: Gallimard, 1981); John Barth, *Letters* (New York: Putnam, 1979); Walter Abish, *Alphabetical Africa* (New York: New Directions, 1974).

3. See Derrida, "Edmond Jabès and the Question of the Book," in *Writing and Difference*, 64: "The passion *of* writing, the love and endurance of the letter itself."

4. Agnès Chalier, "Le Chant de l'absence," *Les Cahiers Obsidiane* 5 (1982): 54.

5. Gabriel Bounoure, "Edmond Jabès ou la guérison par le livre," in *Edmond Jabès*, 66. This essay was first published in 1966.

6. Guglielmi, *Ressemblance*, 41 (Guglielmi's emphasis); see also 100, 170–71.

7. See Derrida, *Writing and Difference*, 65: "And through a kind of silent displacement toward the essential which makes of this book one long metonymy, the situation of the Jew becomes exemplary of the situation of the poet, the man of speech and of writing."

8. Georges Perec, *Un Homme qui dort* (Paris: Union Général d'éditions, 1967), 81–82.

9. See Gershom G. Scholem, *Major Trends in Jewish Mysticism*, 3d ed. (New York: Schocken, 1954), 132–38. I am indebted to my friend and colleague Bruce Erlich for drawing my attention to Abulafia.

10. See, for instance, Bounoure, *Edmond Jabès*, 44: "Remember that Saint Jerome explained to his fervent disciple, Saint Paula, the mysteries contained in each Hebrew letter."

11. Blanchot, "L'Interruption," 870.

12. Adolfo Fernandez Zoïla also speaks of the "weight" of the Jabesian letter. See *Le Livre, recherche autre d'Edmond Jabès* (Paris: Jean-Michel Place, 1978), 90.

13. See Derrida, *Writing and Difference*, 70: "To be a poet is to know how to leave speech. To let it speak alone, which it can do only in its written form." See also Fernandez Zoïla, *Livre*, 55: "It is a question neither of style, nor of savant composition/decomposition, nor of literary procedure, through which modernity might declare itself, but rather of the putting into practice of the principle which says that the written doesn't represent anything, doesn't represent itself, that it presents itself, objectifies itself, exists in and of itself, that it comes to be, finally, as fragment, as major aphorism."

14. See Bounoure, *Edmond Jabès*, 45.

15. Ibid., 65.

16. Scholem, *Major Trends*, 99. See also his article on the Golem in the *Encyclopaedia Judaica*. Other sources for my discussion of the myth include Elie Wiesel, *The Golem*, trans. Anne Borchardt (New York: Summit, 1983), and Georges Perec and Robert Bober, *Récits d'Ellis Island: Histoires d'errance et d'espoir* (Paris: Sorbier, 1980).

17. See DL 128.

18. Edith Dahan, "Le Corps et l'écriture dans *Le Livre des questions*," *Les Cahiers Obsidiane* 5 (1982): 18–19.

19. Jabès discusses this problematic at length in DL 87–101.

20. See Bounoure, *Edmond Jabès*, 51.

21. See, for instance, A 10, 69, 170; EL 7, 15, 23, 26, 36, 50, 58, 73, 75, 89, 98, 105, 110, 115, 121; LR 52; SD 7, 30, 88; P 64.

22. See Robert Duncan, "The Delirium of Meaning," in Gould, ed., *Sin*, 210–11. On Saussure's anagrams, see Jean Starobinski, *Les Mots sous les mots: Les anagrammes de Ferdinand de Saussure* (Paris: Gallimard, 1971).

23. See Scholem, *Major Trends*, 100.

24. Bounoure, *Edmond Jabès*, 36.

25. Guglielmi, *Ressemblance*, 23.

26. See Scholem, *Major Trends*, 135–36.

27. Ibid., 100.

28. Georges Auclair, "Convergences?" *Les Cahiers Obsidiane* 5 (1982): 115.

29. Fernandez Zoïla, *Livre*, 31.

30. See the *prière d'insérer* of *Aely*.

31. Jean Frémon, "Ainsi toujours désignant ce qui manque," *Les Cahiers Obsidiane* 5 (1982): 119.

32. Scholem, *Major Trends*, 132–33.

33. See Georges Perec, *Les Mots croisés* (Paris: Mazarine, 1979), 3–4.

34. See Guglielmi, *Ressemblance*, 122: "Through the exiled letter, silence insinuates itself in the movement of the book and refuses plenitude to the latter."

35. Raymond Queneau is perhaps the staunchest advocate of the mutual complementarity of mathematics and literature. See particularly "Littérature potentielle," in *Bâtons, chiffres et lettres*, rev. ed. (Paris: Gallimard, 1965), 329: "The poet, however refractory toward mathematics he may be, is nonetheless obliged to count up to twelve in order to compose an alexandrine."

36. See Guy-Félix Duportail, "Le Degré 451 de l'écriture," *Les Cahiers Obsidiane* 5 (1982): 83; Scholem, *Major Trends*, 100.

3. THE WORD

1. Fernandez Zoïla, *Livre*, 11.
2. Bounoure, *Edmond Jabès*, 93.
3. See Fernandez Zoïla, *Livre*, 11: "Jabès, man of silence, has often listened to vocables speak, privileging some of them in the obsession of the book that they undermine."
4. See Pierre Missac, "Marge pour deux regards," *Les Cahiers Obsidiane* 54 (1982): 44–53.
5. See Lévy, "Question of Absence," 147–59.
6. Guglielmi, *Ressemblance*, 23.
7. Chalier, "Le Chant de l'absence," 55.
8. See BD 204: "Words taught me to beware of the objects they incarnate." See also Guglielmi, who characterizes Jabès as the "witness of the unreliability of the vocable," in *Ressemblance*, 113.
9. Auclair, "Convergences?" 113.
10. See Bounoure, *Edmond Jabès*, 90: "Ambiguity of poetry: it frees words from their significant form, but it retains the right to bind them, when it must, to a magical form."
11. Fernandez Zoïla, *Livre*, 127.
12. On the Diaspora of words in Jabès, see ibid., 99.
13. See Bounoure, *Edmond Jabès*, 26–27. See also ibid., 88: "The word as a spiritual being, not only possessing a semantic reality, but a substantial sexual reality as well."
14. Ibid., 92–93; Guglielmi, *Ressemblance*, 35.
15. See Fernandez Zoïla, *Livre*, 110: "Words are, for the time being, the supreme stage of human creation; they alone contributed (and continue to do so) to the creation of true human nature."
16. See Waldrop, "Mirrors and Paradoxes," 133–46, esp. 138.
17. See P 43: "In every name, there is a troubling name: Auschwitz."
18. Bounoure, *Edmond Jabès*, 30–33.

19. Ibid., 89.

20. Ibid., 33.

21. See Richard Stamelman, "Nomadic Writing: The Poetics of Exile," in Gould, ed., *Sin*, 94, 99, 105.

22. Ibid., 94.

23. Guglielmi, *Ressemblance*, 191.

24. Eric Gould, "Godtalk," in Gould, ed., *Sin*, 164.

25. See Bounoure, *Edmond Jabès*, 55: "Words were his own resource, the power of his singularity."

26. Guglielmi, *Ressemblance*, 31.

27. See, for example, Bounoure, *Edmond Jabès*, 20: "the incredible kinship of words with the verb."

28. See, for instance, his remarks about his "Judaism after God," in DL 87–89.

29. Gould, "Godtalk," 160–70.

30. Bounoure, *Edmond Jabès*, 60.

31. Guglielmi, *Ressemblance*, 50.

32. Ibid., 176.

4. THE STORY

1. See, for example, the essays in Gould, ed., *Sin*.

2. Paul Auster, "Book of the Dead: An Interview with Edmond Jabès," in Gould, ed., *Sin*, 3–25; Waldrop, "Mirrors and Paradoxes"; Lévy, "The Question of Absence," 5–6, 145, 152–53.

3. This is "apparent" redundancy because the title of the first volume in the septology was adopted for the series as a whole, rather than the contrary.

4. Gerald Prince treats *story* as a subset of *narrative* in *Narratology: The Form and Functioning of Narrative* (Berlin: Mouton, 1982). Personification, problem solving, and a minimal teleology are necessary characteristics of story but not of narrative as a whole. This distinction is productive, especially in a consideration of the narrative technique of Edmond Jabès.

5. Auster, "Book of the Dead," 5–6.

6. Quoted in ibid., 13. The ellipsis is Jabès's.

7. See Jacques Bens, "Queneau oulipien," in Oulipo, *Atlas de littérature potentielle* (Paris: Gallimard, 1981), 23.

8. See, for example, Jabès, "There is such a thing as Jewish writing . . . ," in Gould, ed., *Sin*, 26: "There is no center. There is a point which engenders another point around which an eccentric utterance establishes itself, an interrogation develops. It is the point of no return." Here one can detect the mutual influence of Jabès, Blanchot, and Derrida.

9. See Barthes, *S/Z*, 25–27.

10. On ellipsis as figure in Jabès, see Derrida, "Ellipsis," in *Writing and Difference*, 294–300.

11. See Gérard Genette, *Figures III* (Paris: Seuil, 1972), 251–59.

12. See Roland Barthes, *Essais critiques* (Paris: Seuil, 1964).

13. Quoted in Auster, "Book of the Dead," 17.

14. Quoted in ibid., 12–13.

15. See Jabès, "From the Book of Books to the Books of the Book," *Conjunctions* 6 (1984): 303: "That we are the product of more than one culture is something the question teaches us with its refusal of any fixation, any authoritarian and peremptory answer."

16. Quoted in Auster, "Book of the Dead," 18.

17. Quoted in ibid, 18.

18. Lang, "Writing-the-Holocaust," 194.

19. See Theodor Adorno, *Prisms*, trans. Samuel Weber and Shierry Weber (London: Spearman, 1967), 34.

20. Adorno's reconsideration appears in *Negative Dialectics*, trans. E. B. Ashton (New York: Seabury, 1979), 362: "Perennial suffering has as much right to expression as a tortured man has to scream; hence it may have been wrong to say that after Auschwitz you could no longer write poems."

21. Federman, "Displaced Person," 89.

22. Ibid., 92.

23. Lang, "Writing-the-Holocaust," 191–92.

24. See Jabès, "From the Book of Books to the Books of the Book," 303: "In its hope or its misery, the book proclaims the infinite survival of the sign."

25. Quoted by Jason Weiss in "The Questions of Edmond Jabès," *International Herald Tribune*, 21 July 1983.

26. Auster, "Book of the Dead," 5.

27. Waldrop, "Mirrors and Paradoxes," 142. See also Gould, "Godtalk," 162: "Edmond Jabès writes with such consciousness of the deconstructive play of writing that there is little room for story-telling. Plot fades into self-conscious commentary on the nature of the text, in which the end of writing is the question of writing itself, when words resist the flesh in their strenuous, unending play."

28. See Handelman, "'Torments of an Ancient Word,'" 55–91.

29. Ibid., 59.

30. Yaffa Eliach, *Hasidic Tales of the Holocaust* (New York: Avon, 1982), 136.

31. See Derrida, *Writing and Difference*, 65; Duncan, "Delirium of Meaning," 224: "But in the case of the Jews, since they were the people of a Story, the extermination became a chapter of the Story. And since the Nazis wanted to erase much of the Story of the German spirit, to rewrite and do away with the evidence, they may have been jealous in their hatred of those who were faithful to the Story."

32. Quoted in Auster, "Book of the Dead," 14. See also Blanchot's essay on the fragmentary nature of the Jabesian text, "L'Interruption."

33. See Edward Kaplan, "The Problematic Humanism of Edmond Jabès," in Gould, ed., *Sin*, 124.

34. Jabès, "From the Book of Books to the Books of the Book," 301.

5. THE BOOK

1. Guglielmi, *Ressemblance*, 18.

2. See Fernandez Zoïla, *Livre*, 96: "This dialogue between book and Book constitutes a knot of primordial relations in Jabès's strategy."

3. François Laruelle, "Projet d'une philosophie du livre," *Les Cahiers Obsidiane* 5 (1982): 140.

4. See Lévy, "Question of Absence," 148–49, 154, 157.

5. See Guglielmi, *Ressemblance*, 132.

6. See Handelman, " 'Torments of an Ancient Word,' " 55–91.

7. On Mallarmé and Jabès, see Jean Pfeiffer, "Le Dialogue d'Edmond Jabès," *Les Cahiers Obsidiane* 5 (1982): 108–10.

8. François Laruelle has also noted the double influence of Mallarmé and Blanchot. See his "Projet d'une philosophie du livre," 140.

9. Blanchot, "L'Interruption."

10. See, for instance, "L'Inconditionnel" (CS 87–108); "L'Infaillible décret" (DD 65–66); and "L'Inconditionnel, II" (DD 101–3).

11. See, for example, Y 8, CS 10, and DL 13.

12. Maurice Blanchot, *Le Livre à venir* (Paris: Gallimard, 1959).

13. See, for example, CS 15, CS 51, and PL 20.

14. See, for example, BQ 122, LQ 132: "I talked to you about the difficulty of being Jewish, which is the same as the difficulty of writing. For Judaism and writing are but the same waiting, the same hope, the same wearing out"; and SD 85: "Jew, as figure of exile, of wandering, of strangeness, and of separation; a condition which is also that of the writer." On this theme, see also Derrida, "Edmond Jabès and the Question of the Book," in *Writing and Difference*, 65; and Kaplan, "The Problematic Humanism of Edmond Jabès," 117.

15. See Bounoure, *Edmond Jabès*, 41.

16. See Fernandez Zoïla, *Livre*, 65–66.

17. See, for example, SD 59–60: "Thus my books develop out of time, as in time."

18. See also E 44, and Handelman's excellent analysis of this notion in " 'Torments of an Ancient Word,' " 57–61. See also P 106: "The Jew will be saved by the book that he himself helped to preserve. Perhaps every book is the reborn tale of this rescue."

19. Adolfo Fernandez Zoïla equates Jabès's construct with one of Roland

Barthes, calling the *arrière-livre* the zero degree of the book. See Fernandez Zoïla, *Livre*, 52.

20. See Mary Ann Caws, "Questioning the Question," in Gould, ed., *Sin*, 171–78. An earlier version of this essay was published as "Signe et encadrement: Edmond Jabès ou *Le Livre en question*," in *Les Cahiers Obsidiane* 5 (1982): 74–77. See also Rebellato-Libondi, "Rien ne se crée, rien ne se perd," 111.

21. See Handelman, "'Torments of an Ancient Word,'" 62: "The remarkable achievement of the rabbis—which is so important for Jabès—is to make the Book at once closed and open, already finished yet still to be begun, an open process and yet a graven law."

22. Fernandez Zoïla, *Livre*, 15.

23. The earlier volumes are, in order, *Chansons pour le repas de l'ogre*, *Le Fond de l'eau*, *Trois Filles de mon quartier*, *La Voix d'encre*, *La Clef de voûte*, *Les Mots tracent*, and *L'Ecorce du monde*.

24. See also DL 82: "At first, moreover, I was only thinking of a trilogy."

25. See also the *prière d'insérer* of *Aely*.

26. See Missac, "Marge pour deux regards," 44–53. See also Jacques Derrida, *Margins of Philosophy*, trans. Alan Bass (Chicago: University of Chicago Press, 1982), xxiii: "Can this text become the margin of a margin? Where has the body of the text gone when the margin is no longer a secondary virginity but an inexhaustible reserve, the stereographic activity of an entirely other ear?"

27. Interview with Edmond Jabès, 6 July 1986.

28. The passage quoted is from YE 144, E 42.

29. The passage quoted is from YE 178, E 92–93.

30. A similar passage occurs in DL 21.

31. See, for example, YE 114, Y 160; YE 173, E 85; YE 323, A 157; and LP 23. See also BQ 47, LQ 47: "The Book of the Absent"; BQ 143, LQ 157: "The Book of the Living"; YE 151, E 52: "The Book within the Book"; LR 75: "El-Book"; SD 119: "The Lost Book"; II 92: "The Book of the Dead"; II 96: "The Book of Hidden Narration"; P 105: "The Read Book"; LP 142: "The Read Book."

32. Caws, "Signe et encadrement," 74.

33. Another interpretation of these blank spaces is suggested by Handelman, "'Torments of an Ancient Word,'" 86: "In the early Hebrew texts there was no 'chapter and verse' marking of the Bible; different sections instead were demarcated by the white space between them. The chapter and verse division added by the Jews in the Middle Ages was made necessary by the theological debates forced on the Jews by Christians, who cited chapter and verse."

34. Jean-Pierre Téboul, "La Coupure de la trace," *Les Cahiers Obsidiane* 5 (1982): 12.

35. Bounoure, *Edmond Jabès*, 79.

36. See Guglielmi, *Ressemblance*, 68: "The book is the privileged place of the sign's incontinence and versatility."

37. Jabès evokes the image of writing as crystal elsewhere. See, for example, BY 232, RL 97: "I am certain I exist in the crystal of writings whose luster I could keep in check if I wanted."

38. Jabès alludes repeatedly to "the book within the book"; see, for example, YE 114, Y 161; YE 151, E 52; and II 34–35. See also Guglielmi's remarks on the passage just cited, in *Ressemblance*, 83–85.

39. See Handelman, "'Torments of an Ancient Word,'" 62–63: "For both Jabès and the rabbis, the Book within the Book is also something primordial, a Book not dependent on physical letters, ink, pages, and binding."

40. See Stamelman, "Nomadic Writing," 110: "Writing is the wandering of questions whose unanswerability makes their errancy infinite. The *mise-en-abîme* generated by the perpetual questioning mirrors the endless reflections of writing as it wanders in search of an impossible origin."

41. See also DL 36, "as we write, we are the book."

42. See Dällenbach, *Le Récit spéculaire*, 37–38, 51.

43. Derrida, *Writing and Difference*, 76.

44. See, for example, BY 47, LY 51–52: "It is out of sentences cut down to the very simple (landings on the stairs of half-light) that I have built

my books"; YE 191, E 111–12: "On such a persistent scent we will have built our last dwelling: not a tomb, but the book"; and LR 144: "It is on this nothingness that I have built my books."

6. FIGURES

1. Maurice Blanchot, *Le Dernier Homme* (Paris: Gallimard, 1957).
2. See LD 112.
3. See YE 144, E 42.
4. "Edmond Jabès ou la guérison par le livre," in Bounoure, *Edmond Jabès*, 47–48. The essay was first published in 1966.
5. See Bounoure, *Edmond Jabès*, 109.
6. See Fernandez Zoïla, *Livre*, 141.
7. See Waldrop, "Mirrors and Paradoxes," 134–35: "The seven volumes of *The Book of Questions* are all books about the process of writing a book. Paradox marks nearly all levels of the work, from the literal paradoxes (which are abundant), via the paradoxical use of commentary and metaphor, to the macrostructure of self-reference. I hope to show that *The Book of Questions* takes this structure to a point where what seems play becomes the most radical quest of self-knowledge, and what seems circular opens into an infinite spiral."
8. Fernandez Zoïla has quite correctly characterized ·*(El, ou le dernier livre)* as the "apotheosis" of the point. See *Livre,* 34.
9. See Dahan, "Le Corps et l'écriture dans *Le Livre des questions,*" 26.
10. See ibid., 27: "Diacritical mark in Semitic languages, agent of a particularization in the indefiniteness of language, the point allows us to accede to the legibility of the text (of the subject), to its vocalisation."
11. See LD 112.
12. Perhaps it is this movement that leads Fernandez Zoïla to argue that there is no unique center in Jabès's work, but rather a plurality of centers. See *Livre,* 12.
13. Stamelman, "Nomadic Writing," 93.
14. See Job 13:12 and 30:19.

15. Blanchot, "Interruptions." The essay was first published in 1964.

16. Bounoure, *Edmond Jabès*, 74.

17. See ibid., 39.

18. See Guglielmi, *Ressemblance*, 23, 40, 73–74, 95.

19. Guglielmi, much like Adolfo Fernandez Zoïla, regards the Judaic topos in Jabès's work as a "feigned origin." See ibid., 23: "For it must be said that, for Jabès, a confirmed atheist, *Judaism* and indeed the *cabala* are merely feigned origins, reference points which the work of the book demolishes, cultural locuses emptied and scattered by the book's negative motion." See also ibid., 100, and Fernandez Zoïla, *Livre*, 73–74.

20. Dahan, "Le Corps et l'écriture dans *Le Livre des questions*," 17.

21. Ibid., 16.

22. See Stamelman, "Nomadic Writing," 94.

23. See ibid., 97–98.

24. See Fernandez Zoïla, *Livre*, 39–40.

25. See ibid., 12.

26. See Derrida, "Structure, Sign, and Play in the Discourse of the Human Sciences," in *Writing and Difference*, 278–79.

27. Ibid., 279.

28. Ibid., 280.

b i b l i o g r a p h y

WORKS BY EDMOND JABÈS

Préface aux lettres de Max Jacob à Edmond Jabès. Alexandria:
    Collection Valeurs, 1945.

Chansons pour le repas de l'ogre. Paris: Seghers, 1947.

Le Fond de l'eau. Cairo: La Part du Sable, 1947.

Trois Filles de mon quartier. Paris: G.L.M., 1948.

La Voix d'encre. Cairo: La Part du Sable, 1949.

La Clef de voûte. Paris: G.L.M., 1950.

Les Mots tracent. Paris: L'Age d'Or, 1951.

Paul Éluard. Cairo: La Part du Sable, 1953.

L'Écorce du monde. Paris: Seghers, 1955.

Je bâtis ma demeure: Poèmes 1943–1957. Preface by Gabriel Bounoure. Paris: Gallimard, 1959. Rev. ed. Postface by Joseph Guglielmi. Paris: Gallimard, 1975.

Le Livre des questions. Paris: Gallimard, 1963.

Le Livre de Yukel. Paris: Gallimard, 1964.

Le Retour au livre. Paris: Gallimard, 1965.

Yaël. Paris: Gallimard, 1967.

Elya. Paris: Gallimard, 1969.

Aely. Paris: Gallimard, 1972.

•(El, ou le dernier livre). Paris: Gallimard, 1973.

Ça suit son cours. Montpellier: Fata Morgana, 1975.

Le Livre des ressemblances. Paris: Gallimard, 1976.

Le Soupçon le désert. Paris: Gallimard, 1978.

Du désert au livre: Entretiens avec Marcel Cohen. Paris: Belfond, 1980.

L'Ineffaçable l'inaperçu. Paris: Gallimard, 1980.

Récit. Montpellier: Fata Morgana, 1981.

Le Petit Livre de la subversion hors de soupçon. Paris: Gallimard, 1982.

Dans la double dépendance du dit. Montpellier: Fata Morgana, 1984.

Le Livre du dialogue. Paris: Gallimard, 1984.

Le Parcours. Paris: Gallimard, 1985.

Le Livre du partage. Paris: Gallimard, 1987.

Le Mémoire et la main. Montpellier: Fata Morgana, 1987.

TRANSLATIONS

Elya. Trans. Rosmarie Waldrop. Bolinas, Calif.: Tree Books, 1973.

The Book of Questions. Trans. Rosmarie Waldrop. Middletown, Conn.: Wesleyan University Press, 1976.

The Book of Yukel, Return to the Book. Trans. Rosmarie Waldrop. Middletown, Conn.: Wesleyan University Press, 1977.

A Share of Ink. Trans. Anthony Rudolf. London: Menard, 1979.

The Book of Questions: Yaël, Elya, Aely. Trans. Rosmarie Waldrop. Middletown, Conn.: Wesleyan University Press, 1983.

The Book of Questions: ·El, or the Last Book. Trans. Rosmarie Waldrop. Middletown, Conn.: Wesleyan University Press, 1984.

"From the Book of Books to the Books of the Book." Anon. trans. *Conjunctions* 6 (1984): 301–3.

"If There Were Anywhere But Desert: Selected Poems." Trans. Keith Waldrop. *Denver Quarterly* 19, no. 1 (1984): 3–32.

"There is such a thing as Jewish writing. . . ." Trans. Rosmarie Waldrop. In *The Sin of the Book: Edmond Jabès*, 26–31. Ed. Eric Gould. Lincoln: University of Nebraska Press, 1985.

"At This Unsuspected Boundary." Trans. Rosmarie Waldrop. In *The Sin of the Book: Edmond Jabès*, 32–34. Ed. Eric Gould. Lincoln: University of Nebraska Press, 1985.

"Enlarging the Horizon of the Word." Trans. Rosmarie Waldrop. In *The Sin of the Book: Edmond Jabès*, 35–37. Ed. Eric Gould. Lincoln: University of Nebraska Press, 1985.

"The Question of Displacement into the Lawfulness of the Book." Trans. Rosmarie Waldrop. In *The Sin of the Book: Edmond Jabès*, 227–44. Lincoln: University of Nebraska Press, 1985.

The Book of Dialogue. Trans. Rosmarie Waldrop. Middletown, Conn.: Wesleyan University Press, 1987.

"My Itinerary." Trans. Rosmarie Waldrop. *Studies in Twentieth Century Literature* 12, no. 1 (1987): 3–12.

"From *The Book of Resemblances*." Trans. Rosmarie Waldrop. *Studies in Twentieth Century Literature* 12, no. 1 (1987): 13–25.

The Selected Poems of Edmond Jabès. Trans. Keith Waldrop. Introduction by Paul Auster. Afterword by Robert Duncan. New York: Station Hill Press, 1988.

OTHER WORKS CONSULTED

Abish, Walter. *Alphabetical Africa*. New York: New Directions, 1974.

Adorno, Theodor. *Prisms*. Trans. Samuel Weber and Shierry Weber. London: Spearman, 1967.

———. *Negative Dialectics*. Trans. E. B. Ashton. New York: Seabury, 1979.

Auclair, Georges. "Convergences?" *Les Cahiers Obsidiane* 5 (1982): 113–18.

Auster, Paul. "Book of the Dead: An Interview with Edmond Jabès." In *The Sin of the Book: Edmond Jabès*, 3–25. Ed. Eric Gould. Lincoln: University of Nebraska Press, 1985.

Barth, John. *Letters*. New York: Putnam, 1979.

Barthes, Roland. *Essais critiques*. Paris: Seuil, 1964.

———. *S/Z*. Paris: Seuil, 1970.

Benhamou, Maurice. "Maintenant que quelqu'un vienne. . . ." *Les Cahiers Obsidiane* 5 (1982): 121–22.

Bens, Jacques. "Queneau oulipien." In Oulipo, *Atlas de littérature potentielle*, 22–33. Paris: Gallimard, 1981.

Bilen, Max. "Le Comportement mythique dans l'oeuvre d'Edmond Jabès." In *Jabès: Le livre lu en Israël*, 83–90. Ed. David Mendelson. Paris: Point Hors Ligne, 1987.

Blanchot, Maurice. *L'Espace littéraire*. Paris: Gallimard, 1955.

———. *Le Dernier Homme*. Paris: Gallimard, 1957.

———. *Le Livre à venir*. Paris: Gallimard, 1959.

———. *L'Entretien infini*. Paris: Gallimard, 1969.

———. *L'Amitié*. Paris: Gallimard, 1971.

———. "Interruptions." Trans. Rosmarie Waldrop and Paul Auster. In *The Sin of the Book: Edmond Jabès*, 43–54. Ed. Eric Gould. Lincoln: University of Nebraska Press, 1985.

Bloom, Harold. *Kabbalah and Criticism*. New York: Seabury, 1975.

Bounoure, Gabriel. *Edmond Jabès: La demeure et le livre*. Montpellier: Fata Morgana, 1984.

Cacciari, Massimo. "Black and White." Trans. Roberta Payne. *Studies in Twentieth Century Literature* 12, no. 1 (1987): 73–79.

Cahen, Didier. "En marge de la délivrance." *Les Cahiers Obsidiane* 5 (1982): 134–37.

Caws, Mary Ann. "Signe et encadrement: Edmond Jabès ou *Le Livre en question*." *Les Cahiers Obsidiane* 5 (1982): 74–77.

———. "Questioning the Question." In *The Sin of the Book: Edmond Jabès*, 171–78. Ed. Eric Gould. Lincoln: University of Nebraska Press, 1985.

Chalier, Agnès. "Le Chant de l'absence." *Les Cahiers Obsidiane* 5 (1982): 54–59.

Cohen, Lionel. "*Le Livre des questions*: 'prise de conscience d'un cri.'" In *Jabès: Le livre lu en Israël*, 45–52. Ed. David Mendelson. Paris: Point Hors Ligne, 1987.

Cohen, Marcel. "Lorsqu'une oeuvre. . . ." *Les Cahiers Obsidiane* 5 (1982): 9.

Dahan, Edith. "Le Corps et l'écriture dans *Le Livre des questions*." *Les Cahiers Obsidiane* 5 (1982): 16–36.

Dällenbach, Lucien. *Le Récit spéculaire: Essai sur la mise en abyme*. Paris: Seuil, 1977.

Derrida, Jacques. *Writing and Difference*. Trans. Alan Bass. Chicago: University of Chicago Press, 1978.

———. *Margins of Philosophy*. Trans. Alan Bass. Chicago: University of Chicago Press, 1982.

Duncan, Robert. "The Delirium of Meaning." In *The Sin of the Book: Edmond Jabès*, 207–26. Ed. Eric Gould. Lincoln: University of Nebraska Press, 1985.

Duportail, Guy-Felix. "Le Degré 451 de l'écriture." *Les Cahiers Obsidiane* 5 (1982): 82–92.

Eckhard, Michel. "*Je bâtis ma demeure* d'Edmond Jabès: Ecriture, silence, cri." In *Jabès: Le livre lu en Israël*, 125–28. Ed. David Mendelson. Paris: Point Hors Ligne, 1987.

Elbaz, Shlomo. "Jabès en question." In *Jabès: Le livre lu en Israël*, 139–47. Ed. David Mendelson. Paris: Point Hors Ligne, 1987.

Eliach, Yaffa. *Hasidic Tales of the Holocaust*. New York: Avon, 1982.

Federman, Raymond. "Displaced Person: The Jew / The Wanderer / The Writer." *Denver Quarterly* 19, no. 1 (1984): 85–100.

Fernandez Zoïla, Adolfo. *Le Livre, recherche autre d'Edmond Jabès.* Paris: Jean-Michel Place, 1978.

———. "Le Neutre en devenir chez Edmond Jabès." *Les Cahiers Obsidiane* 5 (1982): 60–63.

Frémon, Jean. "Ainsi toujours désignant ce qui manque." *Les Cahiers Obsidiane* 5 (1982): 119–20.

Genette, Gérard. *Figures III*. Paris: Seuil, 1972.

Goitein-Galperin, Denise-R. "'Mon itinéraire juif. . . .'" In *Jabès: Le livre lu en Israël*, 57–67. Ed. David Mendelson. Paris: Point Hors Ligne, 1987.

Gould, Eric, ed. *The Sin of the Book: Edmond Jabès*. Lincoln: University of Nebraska Press, 1985.

———. "Introduction." In *The Sin of the Book: Edmond Jabès*, xiii–xxv. Ed. Eric Gould. Lincoln: University of Nebraska Press, 1985.

———. "Godtalk." In *The Sin of the Book: Edmond Jabès*, 160–70. Ed. Eric Gould. Lincoln: University of Nebraska Press, 1985.

———. "Epilogue: Jabès and Postmodernism." *Studies in Twentieth Century Literature* 12, no. 1 (1987): 115–23.

Guez-Ricord, Christian-G. "Lettre à Edmond Jabès pour effacer l'adresse." *Les Cahiers Obsidiane* 5 (1982): 8.

Guglielmi, Joseph. "Postface." In Edmond Jabès, *Je bâtis ma demeure*, 325–33. Paris: Gallimard, 1959. Rev. ed. 1975.

———. *La Ressemblance impossible: Edmond Jabès*. Paris: Les Editeurs Français Réunis, 1978.

Handelman, Susan. "'Torments of an Ancient Word': Edmond Jabès and the Rabbinic Tradition." In *The Sin of the Book: Edmond Jabès*, 55–91. Ed. Eric Gould. Lincoln: University of Nebraska Press, 1985.

Israël, Laurence. "Parenthèses et altérité désertique: Une lecture d'Edmond Jabès." In *Jabès: Le livre lu en Israël*, 115–18. Ed. David Mendelson. Paris: Point Hors Ligne, 1987.

Jandin, Pierre-Philippe. "Un Sang d'encre." *Les Cahiers Obsidiane* 5 (1982): 93–100.

Kaplan, Edward. "The Problematic Humanism of Edmond Jabès." In *The Sin of the Book: Edmond Jabès*, 115–30. Ed. Eric Gould. Lincoln: University of Nebraska Press, 1985.

———. "The Atheistic Theology of Edmond Jabès." *Studies in Twentieth Century Literature* 12, no. 1 (1987): 43–63.

Kinczewski, Kathryn. "Reading Disfigured." In *The Sin of the Book: Edmond Jabès*, 179–87. Ed. Eric Gould. Lincoln: University of Nebraska Press, 1985.

Laifer, Miryam. *Edmond Jabès: Un judaïsme après dieu.* New York: Peter Lang, 1986.

Lang, Berel. "Writing-the-Holocaust: Jabès and the Measure of History." In *The Sin of the Book: Edmond Jabès*, 191–206. Ed. Eric Gould. Lincoln: University of Nebraska Press, 1985.

Laruelle, François. "Projet d'une philosophie du livre." *Les Cahiers Obsidiane* 5 (1982): 138–57.

Lévy, Sydney. "The Question of Absence." In *The Sin of the Book: Edmond Jabès*, 147–59. Ed. Eric Gould. Lincoln: University of Nebraska Press, 1985.

Lévy-Valensi, E. Amado. "Le Signe et ses tensions." In *Jabès: Le livre lu en Israël*, 129–35. Ed. David Mendelson. Paris: Point Hors Ligne, 1987.

Macé, Gérard. "La Poésie par défaut." In Gabriel Bounoure, *Edmond Jabès: La demeure et le livre*, 9–16. Montpellier: Fata Morgana, 1984.

Mendelson, David, ed. *Jabès: Le livre lu en Israël.* Paris: Point Hors Ligne, 1987.

———. "Le Mélange (le 'shibbus') des genres." In *Jabès: Le livre lu en Israël*, 41–44. Ed. David Mendelson. Paris: Point Hors Ligne, 1987.

Missac, Pierre. "Edmond Jabès et l'oasis." *Les Nouveaux Cahiers* 36 (1974): 64–68.

———."Marge pour deux regards." *Les Cahiers Obsidiane* 5 (1982): 44–53.

Mosès, Stéphane. "Edmond Jabès: From One Path to Another." Trans. Carol Nappholz and Greg Burkman. *Studies in Twentieth Century Literature* 12, no. 1 (1987): 81–92.

Oulipo. *La Littérature potentielle: Créations, recréations, récréations.* Paris: Gallimard, 1973.

———. *Atlas de littérature potentielle.* Paris: Gallimard, 1981.

Perec, Georges. *Un Homme qui dort.* Paris: Union Générale d'éditions, 1967.

———. *La Disparition.* Paris: Denoël, 1969.

———. *Les Revenentes.* Paris: Julliard, 1972.

———. *Alphabets.* Paris: Galilée, 1976.

———. *Les Mots croisés.* Paris: Mazarine, 1979.

———. *La Clôture et autres poèmes.* Paris: Hachette, 1980.

Perec, Georges, and Robert Bober. *Récits d'Ellis Island: Histoires d'errance et d'espoir.* Paris: Sorbier, 1980.

Petitdemange, Guy. "Edmond Jabès ou le devenir-écriture." *Les Cahiers Obsidiane* 5 (1982): 67–73.

Pfeiffer, Jean. "Le Dialogue d'Edmond Jabès." *Les Cahiers Obsidiane* 5 (1982): 108–10.

Pinhas-Delpuech, Rosy. "Le Désert, le livre: De J. L. Borges à E. Jabès." In *Jabès: Le livre lu en Israël*, 73–81. Ed. David Mendelson. Paris: Point Hors Ligne, 1987.

Prince, Gerald. *Narratology: The Form and Functioning of Narrative.* Berlin: Mouton, 1982.

Queneau, Raymond. *Bâtons, chiffres et lettres.* 1950. Rev. ed. Paris: Gallimard, 1965.

Raczymow, Henri. "Qui est Edmond Jabès?" *Les Cahiers Obsidiane* 5 (1982): 158–67.

Rebellato-Libondi, Chiara. "Rien ne se crée, rien ne se perd." Trans. Arlette Jabès. *Les Cahiers Obsidiane* 5 (1982): 111–12.

Rojtman, Betty. "La Lettre le point." In *Jabès: Le livre lu en Israël*, 95–103. Ed. David Mendelson. Paris: Point Hors Ligne, 1987.

Rolland, Jacques. "Hors du jeu, au plus fort de l'enjeu." *Les Cahiers Obsidiane* 5 (1982): 38–43.

Scholem, Gershom G. *Major Trends in Jewish Mysticism*. 3d ed. New York: Schocken, 1954.

———. *On the Kabbalah and Its Symbolism*. New York: Schocken, 1965.

Shillony, Helena. "Répétitions, ressemblances." In *Jabès: Le livre lu en Israël*, 107–12. Ed. David Mendelson. Paris: Point Hors Ligne, 1987.

Stamelman, Richard. "Edmond Jabès, *Le Livre des questions*." *MLN* 94 (1979): 869–77.

———. "Nomadic Writing: The Poetics of Exile." In *The Sin of the Book: Edmond Jabès*, 92–114. Ed. Eric Gould. Lincoln: University of Nebraska Press, 1985.

———. "On Dialogue and the Other: An Interview with Edmond Jabès." *Studies in Twentieth Century Literature* 12, no. 1 (1987): 27–41.

———. "The Dialogue of Absence." *Studies in Twentieth Century Literature* 12, no. 1 (1987): 93–113.

Starobinski, Jean. *Les Mots sous les mots: Les anagrammes de Ferdinand de Saussure*. Paris: Gallimard, 1971.

———. "Out of this violated mineral night. . . ." Trans. Rosmarie Waldrop. In *The Sin of the Book: Edmond Jabès*, 41–42. Ed. Eric Gould. Lincoln: University of Nebraska Press, 1985.

Téboul, Jean-Pierre. "La Coupure de la trace." *Les Cahiers Obsidiane* 5 (1982): 10–15.

Valvanidis-Wybrands, Harita. "Passer outre." *Les Cahiers Obsidiane* 5 (1982): 78–81.

Waldrop, Rosmarie. "Signs and Wonderings." *Comparative Literature* 27 (1975): 344–54.

———. "Mirrors and Paradoxes." In *The Sin of the Book: Edmond Jabès*,

133–46. Ed. Eric Gould. Lincoln: University of Nebraska Press, 1985.

Weiss, Jason. "The Questions of Edmond Jabès." *International Herald Tribune*, 21 July 1983.

Wiesel, Elie. *The Golem*. Trans. Anne Borchardt. New York: Summit, 1983.

Wellhoff, Jean-Pierre. "L'érotisme du silence." *Revue d'Esthétique* 1 (1978): 126–40.

———. "Une Stratégie de la distraction." *Les Cahiers Obsidiane* 5 (1982): 64–66.

Wybrands, Francis. "La Rumeur, le désastre." *Les Cahiers Obsidiane* 5 (1982): 101–7.

i n d e x

Yukel, tu es mort entre deux mondes ...

(Tu pensais mourir en plein jour ou en pleine nuit.)

Tu es mort entre tes bras que tu as refermés sur toi.

(Sarah garde ses bras ouverts pour faisant quelle étreinte mortelle ?)

Tu es ... la vérité du pacte brisé et ses liens ne savent plus ton nom.

∴

Quelle fut ta vérité, Yukel, et quelle fut celle de Sarah ?

L'amour est une plante vénéneuse où l'injustice ... des hommes ... tourné sur le fouet du despote un motif ... ont arrêté de tourner et l'univers t'a paru aussi plat que la main tendue ... étoile n'était pas plus distante de ta ... ce qu'un doigt d'un doigt ... l'univers t'apparterait ...

... le lieu où il arrêter de tourner pour tourner à son rythme ...

L'heure paraissait libérée de l'heure.

Tu étais rendu à toi-même.

Tu étais ton maître.

Mais étais-tu encore un homme ?

⋯